P9-CBW-127

DEVELOPING LEADERS

DEVELOPING LEADERS

THE TEN KEY PRINCIPLES

John Adair

Talbot Adair / McGraw-Hill Book Company (UK) Limited

The author thanks *International Management* for granting him permission to reproduce three cartoons in Part 2, Chapter 3

British Library Cataloguing in Publication Data

Adair, John, *1934–*
Developing leaders.
1. Management. Leadership – Manuals
I. Title
658.4′092

ISBN 0-07-707076-3

Co-published with the Talbot Adair Press by
McGraw Hill Book Company (UK) Limited
Maidenhead, Berkshire, England

Typeset by Electronic Village, Richmond, Surrey
Printed and bound in Great Britain by
Biddles Limited, Guildford and King's Lynn

Contents

Part Two Some Developments in Leadership Training

Introduction

Good leadership is a country's greatest asset.

DEVELOPING LEADERS has become an issue of importance for a wide variety of organizations today. In times of change and uncertainty there is a clear need for leaders at the top, while the rising expectations of people at work create a need for leadership in every other level of management as well. How can society as a whole, and the organizations and institutions which in part make it up, grow leaders?

This book is an attempt to answer that question. It is made up of two parts. In PART ONE I have put forward the ten key steps or principles of leadership development. Any organization serious about the business of developing leaders should consider adopting them as a practical philosophy.

These principles appeared first in outline in *Effective Leadership* (1983). They remain unaltered, but I have revised them in the light of experience. A recent confirmation of their validity has come from ICI, the first British company to make a billion pounds profit (in 1986). When ICI approached me to help them develop 'manager-leaders' in 1981 they were far from being in such good shape. The experience of working with ICI to apply the principles of leadership development has helped me to refine them and to present them more effectively to a wider audience.

When ICI first contacted me I was the holder of the country's first professorial appointment in Leadership Studies at the University of Surrey, a five year appointment that ended in 1983. During that period I was well-positioned to act as a consultant, guide and friend to new developments in leadership training. PART TWO is a miscellany which includes some 'progress reports' on these new developments. By its nature you may wish to dip into PART TWO according to your particular interests rather read it right through.

This book completes the trilogy of books that I have now written on the broad theme of developing leaders. The first, *Training for Leadership*, was mainly about leadership training at the Royal Military Academy, Sandhurst. In *Action Centred Leadership* I took the story further, and with the help of some twenty contributors I described how the Sandhurst functional leadership course had been adapted for use in industry, how and why it was being used by a variety of organizations, and how it might evolve in the future.

Like its two predecessors *Developing Leaders* is addressed primarily to those involved in the education and training of managers and young people. But I hope that it will also fall — or be put — into the hands of chief executives. For one of my central themes is that developing leaders is a line manager responsibility, and that each chief executive should give a lead — by word and example — in this field. For no strategy, however right, will be implemented by an organization that lacks leadership at the top.

Leaders or Managers — or Both?

> *A well-managed business does not necessarily contain within it the seeds of progress. The organization may be perfect, the methods impeccable, the conditions ideal; but without that extra something, so hard to define yet so potent, today's success might quickly turn into tomorrow's failure.*
>
> *Roger Falk*

The 1960s and 1970s saw the foundation of a number of management colleges in Britain such as the business schools of London and Manchester. The organization that funded them was the Foundation of Management Education (FME).

At the invitation of Philip Nind, its Director, I talked to the Council of the FME in 1981. Are the business schools developing business leaders? That question had clearly arisen in the minds of some members of the Council. As a result, the FME Council asked me to design and lead a day-long seminar for the heads of Britain's business schools on the subject of leadership development. The seminar took place in October 1982 at the London Business School, with about 100 academics and a few managing directors present. Among them was Dick Clayton, who was responsible for management development in GEC (see p. 94). I spoke first on the research into leadership. Then I introduced the hourglass model of career change (p. 39) and the ten principles described below in PART ONE in summary form. Sir John Harvey-Jones, then Chairman of ICI, next gave an outstanding talk on leadership in management. Edgar Vincent, Group Personnel Manager of ICI, complemented it by describing how ICI was going about the work of developing 'manager-leaders' and changing its organizational culture.

The audience was critical and unresponsive. Travelling back to Waterloo Station on a bus I sat next to a dean of one of the business schools, a long-standing acquaintance who had been at the seminar. She gave me a clue to the audience's relative hostility. 'Your ten points of leadership development are what we call *management* development,' she said. It became suddenly clear to me that many business academics were incapable of seeing the difference between leaders and managers, even when they had just heard and seen leadership both eloquently described and exemplified in Sir John Harvey-Jones.

* * *

Since 1979 a spate of American writings has appeared on the difference between leaders and managers which has brought a much wider and deeper awareness of the distinction to Europe. Indeed, American business schools had already begun to recognize what has proved to be a decisive evolution in the concept of management, not a mere 'flavour of the month' or passing fashion.

In February 1983 the Harvard Business School announced that Abraham Zaleznik had been appointed to fill the Konosuke Matsushita Professorship of Leadership, the first chair to be established 'to support research and teaching on the development of effective leadership in society' at Harvard. It was inaugurated in Japan in November 1981, a year before my seminar at the London Business School. Several such appointments in American business schools and universities have been made since. Kenneth Blanchard, for example, became Professor of Leadership at the University of Massachusetts. One college in Pennsylvania wrote to tell me that it had introduced a complete undergraduate course in leadership studies.

The recession in the early 1980s threw into high relief the need for leadership, and those times — who knows — may be passing. But although there was undoubtedly a strong element of fashion or trendiness in the sudden American espousal of leadership, complete with fervent evangelists, after years when the concept was rejected by many of the same academics, the new American books and articles have certainly highlighted some deficiencies in the concept of management as it is currently taught in business schools and management departments. Yet the relation between leadership and management still needs further clarification, a task that I shall attempt in this chapter. If we can be clear about that distinction, then it follows that the relation of developing *leaders* and developing *managers* should fall into place.

ON LEADERSHIP

Leadership is often discussed or analysed in terms of leadership qualities. Some of these qualities, such as intelligence, energy, initiative and enthusiasm are more universal than others. Leaders tend to (or should) exemplify the qualities expected or required in their working groups. A military leader, for example, needs to personify the quality of physical courage, one of a cluster of soldierly virtues.

But leadership is more than a personal attribute, a general quality of personality and character which can be refracted into a spectrum of 'leadership qualities'. It is also a role, determined by the expectations of the group or organization. Studying those expectations allows us to see that there are two strong magnetic poles within them. The expectations arrange themselves like iron filings in response to them. These poles are as follows: the leader is expected to enable the group or organization to fulfil its mission *and* to hold it together as a working unity.

A leader, then, is the kind of person (qualities), with the appropriate knowledge and skill to lead a group to achieve its ends willingly.

This simple concept relates well to the original meaning of lead, which comes from *laed*, a word common to all the old North European languages (Dutch, German, Anglo-Saxon, Norwegian, Danish, Swedish) and more-or-less unchanged within them today. It means a path, road, course of a ship at sea, journey. A leader accompanies people on a journey, guiding them to their destination. By implication he or she holds them together as a group while leading them in the right direction.

ON MANAGEMENT

By comparison with leader and leadership, manager and management are relatively young words. They entered the English language about three or four centuries ago. Their root is the

Latin word *manus*, a hand. The father of our words manager and management was the Italian verb for handling or 'managing' a war horse. English soldiers then brought the words back from the Italian riding schools and applied them to handling armies in the field, handling swords and handling ships. In the 18th and 19th centuries the terms manager and management were applied to employees appointed by entrepreneurs to run their businesses. As owner-entrepreneurs gave way to publicly-owned companies so managers with entrepreneurial and leadership characteristics have been looked for, especially at the more senior levels. The word *director* is very close to leader in meaning.

The first military use of the word management to describe the handling of armies in the field in the English Civil War emerged accidentally from some historical research I once did on that period. It is ironic that I have so often been accused of introducing the military word leadership whereas it turns out that it is management which is originally a military word, like strategy or objectives. By contrast, leadership has no such direct military link.

The current understanding of management, managing and manager is shaped by its use in 18th and 19th century England with reference to managers and under-managers in industry and commerce and, to a lesser extent, within public charitable institutions such as workhouses and boardschools.

What did management mean then? Much as it does now: a body of people responsible for running an industrial or commercial business or a public institution.

Until quite recently an approximate synonym for that activity would be administration. (The first British management school was called the Henley Administrative Staff College.) But now administration seems to have an old-fashioned ring to it. Why is that?

In the first place, the concept of managing has been further developed by focussing much more on objectives that have to be achieved rather than the processes that have to be maintained. The notion that managers are there simply to 'run' a business like a machine no longer sounds quite right. With that, fed by many other sources, has come a much greater emphasis on getting these key results achieved through people.

The two concepts of leading and managing appear to be on converging courses. If both leader and manager were responsible for achieving objectives through other people, what was then the difference? Is leadership — like administration — now a redundant idea?

HOW DO LEADERSHIP AND MANAGEMENT RELATE TO EACH OTHER?

My first thought on this problem, in *Training for Leadership* (1968), was to suggest that leadership is like a raw material that takes different shapes in different fields, and that these shapes are identified by different names. The role that meets the widely-known model of circles of leadership responsibility (task, team and individual – see p. 10) in the military field is what is called *command*; in the ecclesiastical field it is known as *ministry*; and in public life it is called *governance*. In industry and commerce the leadership role is named *management*.

This idea contradicted the reigning orthodoxy. The orthodox view, then as now, is that management is managing all the resources of a business, while leadership is concerned with 'the human resource'. Leadership is merely a sub-set of management. Perhaps my use of the word 'merely' is unfair, because many companies have come to see that managing people is *the* most important activity. 'We are a people business' is repeated so often now that it has become a cliché.

This part/whole solution, as philosophers call it, has been called into question. A reawakening of the spirit of leadership in the difficult years of recession, and the radical questioning of some of the assumptions behind the concept of management, have rendered that traditional or orthodox view obsolete.

What then is the relation of leadership to management? They are distinct, equal and overlapping concepts. It is true that some writers have argued that leadership and management are totally separate concepts with no overlap. But I interpret dichotomizing of this kind as little more than a teaching technique. By polarizing or painting things either black or white, teachers can highlight distinctions which might otherwise go unnoticed. Professors Frederick Herzberg and Douglas McGregor both achieved prominence by advancing theories which polarized things in a black or white way. That is not to say that their theories are necessarily bad, but some distortion is bound to result from such dichotomizing.

THE TWO CONCEPTS GROW TOGETHER

While reviewing and reflecting upon my own work, stimulated by a university professor who came on one of my courses and accused me with teaching management rather than leadership, I came to see that I have blended together leadership and management into a composite concept. This process has taken place subconsciously over a period of two or three decades. The catalyst in the process has undoubtedly been the three circles model. That model now fits in very well into the overlap area between the two concepts. But there remain some distinctive nuances that cling obstinately to each of the two concepts.

One early change made in the three circles model at Sandhurst was to label the second circle 'team maintenance'. This was done on the grounds that the original phrase 'group maintenance' sounded too much like jargon, whereas everyone knew what a team was. There is a much stronger link between teams and teamwork and leaders and leadership than between teams and management.

A second apparently small change made at Sandhurst which opened the door to the synthesis I was evolving was my development of the lists of leadership/membership functions inherited from the American group dynamics movement. Two lists of task and maintenance functions were amalgamated into one and revised in order to relate them more to the real world. They were firmly called leadership functions (see Appendix A). The list could be applied to leadership in organizations as well as in small work groups, but the Sandhurst focus upon groups of platoon size was reflected in the language.

When John Garnett, then Director of the Industrial Society, first came across my work at Sandhurst in applying the three circles and the functional approach to leadership training, he was initially rather dismissive about the functions, I recall. 'That's all old stuff — Fayol and all that,' he said.

Intrigued by the reference I later did some homework on Fayol. Henri Fayol (1841–1925) is regarded as one of the founding fathers of management thought. He was a French mining engineer who became the director of a large group of coal pits before retiring in 1918. His book *Administration Industrielle et Generale* appeared in French in 1916, but was not published in English until 1949.

Fayol divided the activities of an industrial company into six main groups:

Technical	production, manufacture, adaptation.
Commercial	buying, selling, exchange.
Financial	search for and optimum use of capital.
Security	protection of property and people.
Accounting	stocktaking, balance sheet, costs, statistics.
Administration	forecasting and planning, organizing, commanding, coordinating and controlling.

Clearly there was a considerable overlap between Fayol's list of administrative (the nearest French equivalent to the English word managerial) functions in the list above and the list of leadership functions meeting the three circles. The overlap between Fayol's functional understanding and my own is heightened by unpacking what Fayol had to say about the function of 'commanding', a term he obviously borrowed from the French Army (again there is no direct equivalent in French to our words leader or leadership – the French have now imported both our words *leader* and *manager* directly into their language). Fayol defines command as getting the organization going and he gives some examples of what it means in practice. A person in command should:

- Have a thorough knowledge of employees.
- Eliminate the incompetent.
- Be well versed in the agreements binding the business and its employees.
- Set a good example.
- Conduct periodic audits of the organization and use summarized charts to further this review.
- Bring together his chief assistants by means of conferences at which unity of direction and focussing of effort are provided for.
- Not become engrossed in detail.
- Aim at making unity, energy, initiative and loyalty prevail among all employees.

Fayol was the first person to offer a theoretical analysis of management activities. His analysis has withstood more than a half century of critical discussion. Colonel L.F. Urwick, an early British exponent of Fayol's theory in his *The Elements of Administration*, later made much more use of the English word leadership in writing about management. He saw the link clearly between Fayol's work and my own, and — a kind gesture — in 1969 he presented me over lunch with signed copies of all his books on organization and leadership.

To summarize: the core of leadership can be represented in terms of the three circles and the key functions necessary to meet them:

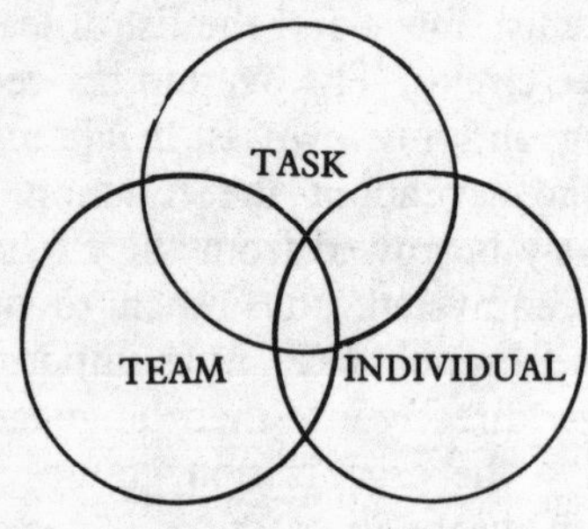

SETTING OBJECTIVES
BRIEFING
PLANNING
CONTROLLING
INFORMING
SUPPORTING
REVIEWING

As we have seen, there is a considerable overlap between this concept of leadership and Fayol's adminstrative activity — labelled 'managing' in English—one of the six general activities listed above which arise in all industrial undertakings. If a careful analysis of Fayol's language is undertaken (for example, *control* has a slightly different connotation in French, where it essentially consists of setting targets in line with the overall plan already decided upon, together with providing information systems to check if the plan is being carried out), the similarity between Fayol's list of functions and my own is even more striking.

Granted this interpretation of leadership, which sees it essentially in terms of role first and personal attributes second, it is legitimate to suggest that management is simply the particular form leadership takes — or should take — in the context of industry, commerce and some of the public services. That is not to say that all managers will see their work in that light: it depends what sorts of views they hold about management and leadership.

CHANGING CORPORATE CULTURE

'Lead, follow, or get the hell out of the way,' is the message which hangs on a wall at United Technologies Corporation, underlining the group's view of managers as leaders.

The notice was quoted by Tom Furtaldo, the director of employee communications at Pratt and Whitney, a division of the American group, who told Britain's National Economic Development Organization's 25th anniversary conference about the role of management development in changing corporate culture.

United Technologies Corporation had to change a 50 year old culture, which was product-oriented, treating people as an expendable resource with managers to control them, to a new culture in which the customer was the centre of the universe, quality was built in, rather than achieved through inspection, and where people were the single most important part of the organization.

"The fundamental purpose of management is not to control but to get out of the way, to encourage people and take initiatives and risks and support them when they fail," he said.

To achieve this, the company had to overhaul its policies and procedures and change management thinking. To develop its managers, it set up a programme to inculcate the idea of managers as leaders. It ran mandatory training courses, which developed a feeling among managers that everyone in the company shared the burden of making a success of it, and that initiative was to be encouraged.

Douglas McGregor suggested in *The Human Side of Enterprise* that organizations and managers could be divided into those that held a low view of man (Theory X) and those who held a high view (Theory Y). Those who hold a high concept of man, as McGregor did, do tend to see management as synonymous with leadership. American writers such as Chester Barnard in his book *The Functions of the Executive* and Peter Drucker in *The Practice of Management*, and British writers — notably L.F. Urwick in *Leadership in the 20th Century* and Roger Falk in *The Business of Management* — all laid considerable stress on leadership within management. The experience of the Second World War, and the influence of such powerful advocates of leadership in management as Lord Slim further encouraged those who adopted what I have called the high view of management.

* * *

The fragments of a different concept of management still persist. In order to understand it one must remember that managers and under-managers in the 19th century were selected largely from the ranks of the professional classes already employed by the entrepreneur-owners; principally they were drawn from engineers and accountants. Now engineers were seen — perhaps unfairly — to be concerned with machines; accountants with figures. Both were systems-minded.

This reliance upon systems (and ultimately upon a more scientific approach), stemming from the dominance of engineers and accountants in the early days of running industrial organizations, gives the concept of management today one of its most important nuances — one that is absent from the concept of leadership. But, as each generation discovers for itself, systems are only half the solution: the other half are the people involved in working the system.

Those early managers in the 19th century and their successors transferred their mechanistic assumptions to the problem of managing 'hands'. They saw humans as things, cogs in a system. The organization as a whole was a machine which they, the managers, were 'running'. This mechanistic philosophy of 'scientific management' is forever associated with an American engineer Frederick W. Taylor, whose influence was most potent between 1905 and 1917.

Setting aside Taylor's view of man, his work does mark a stage in the development of the management concept. The functions of *planning* and *controlling* were heavily emphasized in his work. Above all the introduction of systems and systematic thinking — the application of science to management — held out the promise of increasing productivity.

The concept of management has acquired some definite undertones or connotations over the two or three centuries of its existence, largely from its formative years in the last century, nuances which cling to it like a comet's tail. Some of these are now widely thought to be questionable, such as the mechanistic doctrines of human nature and organization.

On a more positive note, a strong overtone of *administration*, especially financial administration, still remains implicitly or explicitly related to *management*. I think that being a good manager implies that you are a good administrator.

THE ESSENCE OF MANAGEMENT

In *Summer Lightning*, P.G. Wodehouse dubs Lord Emsworth's secretary 'the efficient Baxter':

> We have called Rupert Baxter efficient and efficient he was. The word, as we interpret it, implies not only a capacity for performing the ordinary tasks of life with a smooth firmness of touch, but in addition a certain alertness of mind, a genius for opportunism, a genius for seeing clearly, thinking swiftly and Doing It Now.

Leadership also has some distinctive overtones. To begin with *change* and *leadership* are two closely related concepts. Change tends to highlight the need for leadership; conversely leaders are likely to create change even where others do not see the need for it. Managers are sometimes seen as being there to achieve the objectives set by others (owners, directors). Leaders are seen to be responsible for new objectives and aims, against a background of thinking through the interplay of the fundamental purpose of the organization and its changing, challenging environment.

Other significant nuances of leadership have been discovered — or rediscovered — in the last ten years. Managers often motivate by balancing rewards and threats; their ways of motivating others may even border on the manipulative. Leaders also reward and punish on occasions, but they also lead by example; they *inspire* confidence and they generate in others a genuine enthusiasm and commitment for the work in hand. 'You can be appointed a manager,' it has been said, 'but you are not a leader until your appointment is ratified in the hearts and minds of those who work for you.'

⋆ ⋆ ⋆

In summary: the relation between managing and leading is an overlapping one. Neither concept must push the other out of existence. Managing at its best is much the same as leading as understood in the functional approach. A manager is often — but not always — a leader in industry or commerce. Like all leaders he or she is also a colleague and a subordinate; the team membership role is equally necessary and positive. No leadership exists in the raw: it is always incarnated in a situation. A business leader needs technical and financial knowledge: he or she must also exemplify the qualities required by those who work in that field. A leader of managers should personify the qualities of a good manager. These include the distinctive management virtue of being a good administrator of such resources as money, property and time. A manager will also respect and use systems, for the balance between order and freedom is the essence of organization. Leadership has certain overtones — a sense of direction, vision and inspiration — which are now relevant in management at all levels.

THE MANAGER–LEADER

I'm just a hired hack — a professional manager. I'm proud of that — I'm not a proprietor, not dominant. I lead by example and persuasion and a hell of a lot of hard work. Not on the basis of power or authority. My skills are to help a large number to release their energies and focus themselves. It is switching on a lot of people and helping them achieve a common aim. People only do things they are convinced about. One has to create conditions in which people want to give of their best.

The board of directors should be, in Nelson's phrase, a band of brothers. We should be so aware of one another's views that any one of us could act for the lot of us.

Sir John Harvey-Jones

LEADERSHIP OR MANAGEMENT DEVELOPMENT?

With this discussion in mind you may be able to see why it is tempting to give in to the times and call it all management development. Many of the readers of this book will be reading it with industrial and commercial organizations in mind. The paths of management development and leadership development will run together for most of the career journey, especially in the middle stages. But the concept of leadership development has to be retained. For it is arguably wider and deeper than the concept of management development.

Another reason for resisting the clutches of management development is that its exponents have managed to make it sound so dull and boring. Leadership development is not free from jargon, but the language is so straightforward that any chief executive or line manager can grasp the principles and relate them to the strategic future of the enterprise. For, as one chief executive said to me, 'Developing leaders is far too important to be left to the personnel department.'

KEYPOINTS

- Leading and managing can overlap so considerably in times of change and uncertainty that they come to mean much the same thing.
- The three circles — achieving the task, building the team, and developing/motivating each individual — and the accompanying leadership functions, close the gap considerably between the two concepts.
- Leadership has five distinctive nuances not found in management. It implies a sense of direction, teamwork, inspiration, example and acceptance by others.
- Management also has overtones. These include a belief in and application of systems, the belief in scientific method, a stress on planning, monitoring and controlling, and a stress on good administration.
- Both concepts have 'blind spots'. Managing can be mechanistic and over-concerned with controls. Leadership does not necessarily imply any organizational or administrative abilities. Moreover, a strong leader can take people in the wrong direction. Leadership needs to be kept in perspective: it is not the only ingredient of success.
- Management is prose; leadership is poetry.

Changing things is central to leadership. Changing them before anyone else is creative leadership.

PART ONE *Developing Leaders in Ten Steps*

1 A Strategy For Leadership Development

A business short on capital can borrow money, but a business short on leadership has little chance of survival.

Field-Marshal Lord Montgomery leaned forwards across the lunch table. 'What is the first rule of strategy?' he demanded. 'You won't find it in any book. I learned it by hard experience.'

Needless to say, Monty did not need much encouragement to supply his own answer! It went as follows:

> *The commander-in-chief must be sure that what is strategically desirable is technically possible with the resources at his disposal.*

A decade later I recalled these words. A chief executive of a major company sat across the lunch table. He told me about a disastrous attempt at diversification. 'I learned by hard experience,' he said, 'that it's no good taking over a company if you don't have management expertise in that field — we were way out of our depth.'

People, especially managers, are the key resource of a business enterprise. What is strategically desirable cannot be achieved unless the people available have the necessary knowledge, training and skill to make it happen.

Therefore alongside its corporate strategy for the future a board of directors needs what could be called a 'people plan'. Without a strategy for growing leaders for tomorrow — the corporate strategy will remain a merely paper projection. Strategy and people — the key resource — go together. It is people that make things happen.

A people strategy at boardroom level should embrace everyone who works for the enterprise, not just leaders or managers. As well as management development it should encompass policies on remuneration and rewards, safety at work, communications, industrial relations, as well as technical and professional training at all levels. Important though these ingredients in the overall strategy are, they lie outside the scope of this book.

Although one often hears lip-service paid to the importance of people in industry it is significant that 'personnel' still comes fairly low on the agenda of most boards of directors. Why is this the case? It is worth reflecting on that strange fact.

One possible answer is that personnel executives have failed to reach the policy-making jobs they seek. The result is a continuing difficulty in attracting the right recruits, as the profession is not seen as a passport to the board. And so it becomes a vicious circle. In some cases, the reorganization of companies has meant that responsibilities for manpower planning and training have even been hived off to other departments, leaving personnel managers with the tasks of salary administration, ensuring that statutory obligations and social issues — such as race relations, sex discrimination and unfair dismissals — are taken into account, smoothing the introduction of new technology, and handling carefully the sensitive matter of redundancies. Industrial relations, the jewel in the crown of personnel management in the 1970s, has faded into the background, and the development of people — now the essence of the role — has not yet replaced it in the minds and hearts of many personnel executives.

Many personnel managers have failed to move from being 'systems administrators' to 'creative consultants', or — to drop that jargon — they have been managers and not leaders. They are ill-equipped to understand the business and poorly placed to grasp the corporate strategy. Personnel professionals who, by contrast, have established close links with senior and line managers are usually able to make recommendations that are directly geared to the needs of the business. They correspondingly enjoy a much higher level of acceptance than their more traditional colleagues in other companies.

* * *

There are plenty of signs of change. Guest, Keen and Nettlefolds, the automotive components and engineering group, recently modified the structure of responsibilities of its main executive board to make the company better suited to the way its separate businesses are developing. The management of 'human resources' has been given main board status, a reflection of what GKN says is a commitment to training and executive development. 'These changes are designed to bring our organizational operation more in tune with strategic thinking,' says the managing director.

Although many personnel managers would envy GKN's new 'human resources director' his seat on the main board I wonder how many would know what to do if they got there. A key responsibility, I suggest, would be for the 'human resources director' to persuade his or her colleagues, especially the chief executive, to adopt a strategy for developing leaders.

Such a strategy would not only fit in with the existing corporate plan, so that the task needs of the business were being met. The development of entrepreneurial leaders, if successful, could also open up new strategic vistas. It's amazing what you can do if you have the right people. Opportunity will not find such a company ill-prepared.

THE STRATEGIC IMPERATIVE

Companies cannot just stand still. Remember in *Through the Looking Glass*, when Alice asks the Red Queen why all the people are running around—so unlike her homeland where everyone took their time. 'A slow sort of country,' said the Queen. 'Now, *here*, you see, it takes all the running you can do, to keep in the same place. If you want to get somewhere else, you must run at least twice as fast as that!' The same applies to companies—they have to grow to survive and prosper.

KEYPOINTS

- What is strategically desirable is not always technically feasible. Usually it is not shortage of money or equipment, but the calibre and knowledge of managers that limits what can be done.
- To build up the strategic capability of an enterprise — its capacity to grow and change, to move forwards along planned lines — you must upgrade the professional and technical capability of its people.
- An essential factor in success is the quality of leadership shown at every level in the enterprise.
- There should be a strategy for leadership or management development, hammered out and then ratified in the boardroom.
- You can develop leaders in an organization up to a certain point without the commitment of the board, but beyond that point the exercise is doomed to frustration and failure.
- It is the responsibility of the personnel or 'human resources' director to persuade his line colleagues that they are accountable for the third circle — 'developing the individual' — in the context of the common strategy and the evolving organization.

> *Business is about leadership; it requires understanding, courage, single mindedness, drive and an ability to persuade and lead others. To manage change one often needs to change managers ... particularly managers who fail to involve their people and so secure their full commitment.*
>
> *Sir Michael Edwardes*

2 Selection

> *It is important for everyone to believe, whether they succeed or not, that success is linked with some kind of logic and beholden to some notion of legitimacy.... To put it another way, it is psychologically intolerable, having risen to the heights, to be badgered by doubt that you do not really deserve it.*
>
> *Alistair Mant*

Even the best gardener cannot turn a tulip into a rose, but a horticulturist can improve a tulip. Selection — choosing people with the potential for leadership — is the next key principle to be considered.

For individuals vary in their potential for leadership — defined here as the ability to enable a group to achieve its task, to build or maintain it as a team, and to motivate, inspire and develop each person in it. Some have a naturally high aptitude for leadership and others a very low aptitude. You cannot take the latter and turn them into the former. Most managers — or would-be managers — fall somewhere in the middle range of the continuum. Any organization which means business must ensure that it gains its fair share of potential leaders. In short, it needs a method of selecting men and women with potential as leaders.

THE RIGHT PERSON FOR THE RIGHT JOB

Selection can be roughly divided into two parts. First, there is the selection of new recruits from outside the organization. Some of these may be applying directly for management jobs. Others, seeking specialist appointments in the first instance, may blossom into managers later. Many of these appointments will be made from the ranks of graduates looking for their first job in industry, commerce or the public services.

Secondly, the principle of selection applies to internal appointments, notably promotions. It is not always easy to judge whether or not a person who has shown leadership at one level is capable of exercising leadership at the next level. Many a manager is still promoted to the level of his or her incompetence.

MANAGEMENT AND LEADERSHIP SELECTION

When selecting anyone for a leadership position (assuming that the role of leader — task, team and individual — is the core of the specifically managerial responsibility) one is looking for two sets of potential abilities: the general or transferable leadership talents and the more situation-related aptitudes and knowledge required for leadership to be exercised effectively in a specific field.

It is beyond the scope of this book to discuss the second set of more specific requirements. Obviously a candidate for a regular commission in the Army has to have a high standard of physical fitness, and that can be tested. A candidate for a commission as a pilot in the Royal Air Force must pass a set of stringent aptitude tests — I remember failing in my attempt to join a university air squadron because I was slightly colour blind. There should be equivalent industry-specific tests for those who aspire to lead in any field. The selection of potential managers for profit-making industry or commerce is no exception. Numeracy, for example, and some aptitude for using information technology, should be tested. In that sense, selecting potential or actual business executives for appointments is bound to be wider than selecting them purely and simply as leaders. Other factors clearly have to be taken into account.

The most common method of selecting people for jobs is still the interview. Paradoxically, it is also the method which has the most question marks against it.

In the first year of the Second World War the British Army relied upon the interview for choosing officers. Twenty-five per cent (and in one case fifty per cent) of those picked out by this way were subsequently returned to their units from the officer training schools as being unfit to lead platoons.

Alarmed by this high rate of failure and its effects on the individuals concerned, the Adjutant-General of the day, Sir Ronald

Adam, assembled a working party of senior officers and psychologists. Together they devised a new method of selecting leaders, called the War Office Selection Board Interview — universally known by its acronym WOSBI (pronounced Wosbee). It was the grandfather of all the assessment centres we know today.

The WOSBI was spread over several days. It was based upon the principle of selecting leaders *for* groups by placing candidates *in* groups with tasks to perform. The selectors then watched how far each candidate performed the necessary functions to help the group to achieve its task and to hold it together as a working unity. (For a fuller account of the method, and the early form of the functional approach to leadership behind it, see my *Training for Leadership.*)

The WOSBI system was a spectacular success and it is still used by the British Army and the other armed services who soon adopted it. The US Marine Corps also borrowed it, as I saw for myself when I visited their officer training school at Quantico. Apart from the Civil Service, which introduced its own version of the WOSBI, hardly any other organization showed interest in this method of selection. Then a rash of assessment centres catering for industry and commerce made their appearance on both sides of the Atlantic. The full potential of this method, however, has yet to be realized by industry and commerce, education and the public services.

No one method by itself is sufficient. There is no single scientifically perfect method of assessing leadership. Therefore it is best to rely upon a combination of two or more imperfect methods. Done properly and taken together, they will give one a good reading on any individual candidate. Let us review them briefly.

INTERVIEWS

Interviews can range from fairly unstructured meetings to those where planned and specific questions are asked. More than one interviewer may be involved.

Successive studies of the value of interviews have confirmed the British Army's conclusion, namely that they are poor tools for predicting leadership performance.

The greater use of panel interviews has led to some improvement in the quality, although of course much still depends upon who is on the panel. Also the introduction of job-related incidents — asking the candidate how he or she would respond in a given situation—also produces some relevant data. A more sophisticated version of it — already in use for the selection of some non-commissioned officers — has these incidents on video tape, with the candidate asked to choose between different courses of action.

Interviews are simple, convenient and cheap, but they are also time-consuming and therefore should not be used for initial screening. Training in interviewing skills is essential if adverse subjectivity — such as the well-known 'halo' and 'horns' effects — is to be avoided or at least controlled. For people do have a tendency to appoint people like themselves without being aware of this unconscious bias.

PSYCHOLOGICAL TESTS

Psychological tests fall into two main categories: those testing mental abilities such as the general IQ and specific abilities or aptitudes, and personality/interest questionnaires designed to yield data about the temperament, disposition and attitudes of the candidate.

Cognitive tests have a useful part to play in checking suitability for a range of occupations, as already mentioned. The evidence about personality tests is much more in dispute. In the context of leadership, I know of no questionnaire-type personality test which has any established validity as an indicator of leadership potential or performance.

BIODATA AND REFERENCES

Biographical data, or biodata, begins with the collection of the information found on most application forms — date of birth, educational record, employment record, and interests. More sophisticated methods include the use of biodata questionnaires with more than 100 questions.

Although it is an obvious point it is worth stressing that a person's 'track record' is often a good indicator of leadership potential, especially for internal or post-experience appointments from outside. Even with young people, who by definition do not have much of a track record, biodata can throw up some useful clues. Whether or not a graduate has taken any leadership role in school, university or the community, for example, will appear on a carefully-worded application form. Such positions usually involve election, a primitive but nonetheless valuable indicator of how the young person's peers have rated him or her as a leader.

The value of references is generally thought to be low. Still, they can be used as a basis for discussion with candidates and/or as a final check on a candidate before he or she is offered a job.

LEADERSHIP ASSESSMENT CENTRE

An assessment centre based upon the WOSBI principle of putting candidates into small groups with a variety of tasks to do, sometimes without an appointed leader and sometimes with one, would undoubtedly be the most comprehensive and specific method for attempting to identify leadership potential or to predict future leadership performance. I am assuming that the core group selection method would be buttressed by panel interviews, a small battery of individual exercises, using interactive videos, of the situation-response type, and some cognitive tests — possibly a personality test as well — to provide some discussion points.

Such a leadership assessment centre would be time-consuming and relatively expensive to run. Only a small number of candidates can be covered by a single panel, and at least one day would be needed. It usually only makes sense for very large organizations with a need to assess many applicants — such as the armed forces — to have their own assessment centres.

It is worth noting, however, that many large organizations who have established assessment centres have not done so with leadership as the main ingredient. In other words, the leadership selection element in these corporate assessment centres is fairly minimal.

Should a national leadership assessment centre, based upon WOSBI principles, be established for industry, commerce and the public services? There is certainly a case for such a centre, if only to be a 'centre of excellence' where selectors could be trained, research and development carried out, and national standards set.

In any good leadership assessment experience there is an element of training or development, just as in leadership training there is often inevitably a small element of selection. Since assessment centres often incorporate work sample/situation tests they do provide candidates with a taste of the job and an opportunity for self-assessment.

Although there is little to be said for the idea of self-assessment centres on their own, the decision to apply for a job and a decision to accept a job both entail a degree of self-assessment and a comparison of oneself with the requirements and characteristics of the job. The more realistic the job preview, the easier this process can be.

For at their best assessment centres look *forward* by checking how candidates will perform in conditions which simulate future jobs. This is an advantage over interviews which look at performance in *past* jobs, none of which may be anything like tomorrow's possible job.

One last point on assessment centres: selecting the selectors — and training them — is vitally important. Psychologists should be responsible for the more technical aspects of processing and interpreting any questionnaires used. Among the line managers or their equivalents — a few seconded to this work but most drawn from a panel of trained leadership selectors — make sure that there are plenty who have established themselves as leaders. Warn them against the danger of choosing too many 'safe' and unexciting candidates. Who knows what changes, chances and uncertainties for the organization lie ahead? Choose leaders for tomorrow as well as leaders for today.

INTERNAL SELECTION — THE SELF-DEVELOPMENT APPROACH

If one examines how individuals have 'got on' in organizations one finds that they have developed themselves. That is to say they have:

- Applied themselves to fully understanding all the ramifications of their job.

- Equipped themselves for advancement by study, i.e. by sitting for examinations and wide reading.
- Ensured that, by one means or another, they have acquired the right sort of experience for effectively holding down more senior jobs.

Because companies start on the assumption that they are developing their managers, they spend a great deal of effort trying to identify those with potential — in particular the 'fast growers', with a view to spending time and money on their future development. Clearly the whole task would be simpler and more effective if those who thought they had potential identified themselves to the company and this is exactly the system that the Services operate.

Organizations, however, can still very much influence affairs. Firstly, by the emphasis they place on senior managers helping their subordinates to develop and secondly, by spending the money and allowing the time for a manager to undertake further training, e.g. attendance at an external course.

Reference has been made to the system adopted by the Services in which, in effect, the individual with promotion in mind is required to identify himself. For instance a young officer (a junior/middle manager) who wants senior command (senior management), knows that this is most unlikely unless he passes in to Staff College (General Management Course). He also knows he won't get there unless he studies for it and passes the necessary examinations. He is not sent to the Staff College. He equips himself to go there.

Self-identification of potential could not be adopted wholesale in many kinds of organization — practical reasons alone would rule it out. Nevertheless there is a strong case in larger companies for adopting the principle for those who consider they are 'fast growers', especially those in the all-important under 40 age group. This could be brought about by requiring junior/middle managers to apply for attendance at general management courses. Selection could be by a selection board of senior managers and directors. One of the major by-products of this system would be that directors would get to know personally the young, ambitious and effective managers within the company.

KEYPOINTS

- An accurate assessment of leadership potential — a prediction of probable performance in terms of the task, team and individual — comes from placing people in working groups and seeing what they do.
- Such a group approach to leadership selection should be the core of the initial selection process for those aspiring to be leaders who have passed the first screening, supported by full biodata, interviews, industry-related tests and psychological tests.
- Selection procedures should be so designed that they enable people to assess their own strengths and weaknesses. People should be encouraged to assess their own suitability for a particular job or field of work.
- Selectors should be chosen carefully from line managers with a proven track record as managers of people at work. Some initial training in selection methods should be given them.
- The principles of leadership selection should apply to internal appointments. People should be required to apply for promotion and submit themselves to a selection board which is fair and seen to be fair.

Nobody doubted his capacity to rule until he became Emperor.

Tacitus (on Galba)

3 Training for Leadership

> *Training is everything. The peach was once a bitter almond; cauliflower is but cabbage with a college education.*
>
> *Mark Twain*

Selection procedure, however good, will only identify and to some extent measure a person's natural *potential* for leadership. That potential has to be developed. Leadership training has an important role to play in that process.

Training is simply a form or method of teaching, the imparting of information or skill so that others may learn. Training stresses instruction with a specific end in view. Both training and instruction have become unfashionable words in the worlds of management education and management development, perhaps because they have undertones for some people of learning drills or of rather methodical and formal teaching. But training need not have these associations. Nor need it be tied to classroom work. Its basic meaning here is to enable people to learn leadership so as to fit or qualify them to lead.

LEADERSHIP TRAINING AT SANDHURST

At the Royal Military Academy Sandhurst a breakthrough was made in leadership training which has had wide repercussions. As I have written extensively about it in my other books, notably *Training for Leadership*, I shall resist the temptation to do more than outline this development here.

Until 1960 leadership training at Sandhurst consisted mainly of a series of talks given by company commanders to the officer cadets, followed by discussion. The briefs for the talks reflected exclusively the qualities approach to leadership.

As a result of various experiments I was able to demonstrate the value of the functional approach in such a way as to persuade my military colleagues that the Sandhurst leadership syllabus would benefit from the introduction of a concentrated thirty-six hour course along functional leadership lines.

Apart from introducing to the officer cadets the situational and group or functional approaches to leadership – the three circles and key leadership functions – the new course differed from the old syllabus in the methods it employed. For example, instead of discussion following the instructor's talk it preceded it. In the first session the officer cadets were asked to divide into small groups of five and to answer the question 'What is leadership?' They came back with their replies written up on flipchart paper for critical comparison in plenary session.

In other words, the officer cadets were being invited to draw upon their own experience and to think for themselves. This method of using small groups in training, and of putting discussion *before* instruction, was revolutionary then although it had since become commonplace. Even flipcharts had yet to be invented: we used large loose sheets of white paper and felt pens, which had only just appeared on the training scene.

After a brief talk from the company commander on the qualities, situational and functional approaches to leadership, with the first introduction of the three circles on a chart (the use of the overhead projector was not then widespread), the officer cadets went outside into the extensive grounds of Sandhurst and tackled a series of three outdoor leadership exercises of the WOSBI type. While one group with a leader tackled the task, however, the other groups – armed with millboards and a list of the key leadership functions (see Appendix A) – observed the leader's actions. After each exercise there was a review or debrief on the leadership aspect in which all were encouraged to join.

A further indoor session looked at the decision-making continuum as a means of bridging the gap between non-military and military leader. In a short talk the instructor emphasized the influence of the characteristic working situation – in this case the battlefield – upon the degree to which the leader can share decisions with his subordinates.

In the evening all the officer cadets doing the course – about 250 each time divided among 12 companies – came together to see the feature film 'Twelve O'Clock High' (which I managed to obtain from America with considerable difficulty, having seen a poor copy of it shown at a day's seminar on leadership organized by the Royal Marine Commandos in Plymouth a year or two earlier – 'it's the best film on leadership,' the brigadier had assured me. He was right.) The film was stopped after the first leader in it gets sacked. The officer cadets were asked first to say why – in light of the three circles – he had failed and, secondly, what they would do if they took over the unit portrayed in the film. The discussion following the film often continued until late into the night.

Next morning there were two sessions. 'Exercise Remake' was essentially a case study about a unit in peacetime where morale was low. Again the officer cadets were asked what they would do as leaders in order to put things right. They role-played their solutions, representatives from each small group of five taking the parts of platoon commanders and presenting their proposals to an experienced company commander.

In the final application session the officer cadets tackled three questions:

- What have you learnt on this course?
- What do you still need to know more about?
- How can you apply what you have learnt?

After the small groups had reported back – for time reasons they were restricted to three answers to each question – everyone filled in an evaluation form. Apart from giving some immediate feedback to the company commander running the course, the evaluation sheets enabled me as Adviser on Leadership Training to keep a check on quality. In one or two instances, for example, it was clear that a particular session had not gone well, and I was usually able to sort out the problem.

* * *

Once the functional leadership course was firmly established the next step was to extend leadership training into the field. Basically this was done by adding a leadership debrief to the tactical debriefs during field exercises. In order that this change should be introduced I had to demonstrate first that the field training in tactics on long exercises at home or abroad was not training leaders and that it could be made to do so. When the functional approach was introduced into the field training of future platoon commanders the results were impressive (see *Training for Leadership*, Chapter Six, where I quoted extensively from what officer cadets said they had learnt.)

The changes at Sandhurst were made without much staff training in any formal sense. Sandhurst then operated a gentlemanly form of what I later heard described as 'sitting by Nellie'. New company commanders and company instructors would overlap with their predecessors and pick up the reins from them. On the whole that system worked well with the twelve company commanders, who tended to be outstanding officers anyway. The sixty or seventy company instructors (usually captains) who were responsible for field leadership training varied widely in their effectiveness as leadership trainers, from excellent to average or indifferent. Perhaps that was inevitable in the early days of the experiment.

EVALUATION

Evaluation of training is never easy. There is no simple infallible indicator. Post-course evaluation by students, for example, sometimes reflects enthusiasm for the participative and enjoyable methods used on the course. Therefore I identified five criteria – each imperfect by itself – which should be used:

- immediate post-course evaluation sheets.
- evidence that lessons have been applied at work.
- post-course evaluation a year or more later.
- the judgement of experienced practitioners.
- the judgement of specialists.

At Sandhurst the field tactical exercises over what was then a course lasting two years gave us plenty of opportunity to see if the officer cadets were transferring their learning about leadership into practice. Field leadership training was seen as a stepping stone. It allowed us to reinforce the basic message in a variety of more realistically military situations, so that transfer was facilitated.

Post-course evaluation a year or more later was not possible until the first officer cadets to undertake a functional leadership training at Sandhurst had been commissioned and had served with their units for some time (most arms, such as armoured and artillery, had further technical training courses for new second-lieutenants). Later I sent a questionnaire to a cross section of 100 young officers who had been the officer cadets of Intakes 35 and 36. In *Training for Leadership* (pp. 145-9) I quoted from 12 of the 70 replies I received to illustrate the long-term effectiveness of the new course.

As to the judgement of experienced practitioners, it is clear that the functional leadership course could not have been introduced at Sandhurst unless it had successfully passed the scrutiny of many practical military leaders. Their evaluation of the content of the course, their endorsement from experience of the message, is an important ingredient in evaluation.

Lastly, I have always advocated asking specialists to evaluate leadership training. For I know that sometimes - despite enthusiastic participants, ecstatic tutors, dazzled line managers, and extravagant reports of transformations overnight - I have been instinctively aware that something is wrong with a course. Leadership courses, like shiny second-hand motorcars, can be remarkably impressive until you get a mechanic to have a look under the bonnet. A specialist in any field should have an educated instinct. But specialists in management development or in educational techniques are not infallible. Their judgement is only one factor among the five I have listed. Experts, it has been said, should be kept on tap but not on top. That principle certainly applies when it comes to evaluating leadership training.

HALLMARKS OF EFFECTIVE TRAINING

The success of leadership training at Sandhurst in the 1960s was not a matter of chance. Later I identified certain principles which were consciously applied. With more experience I have come to recognize them as the hallmarks of effective leadership training, and indeed many other kinds of training as well. Therefore these short notes are general in character:

SIMPLE	The content of the course should be simple. It should concentrate on what *must* be learnt, as opposed to the *should* and *might* areas. There should be a lack of unnecessary complications and management or psychological jargon.
PRACTICAL	The approach should be essentially practical, focussing on the actions of leadership. There should be no abstractions or theory for its own sake.
PARTICI-PATIVE	When people are talking they are thinking; they learn by doing and reviewing what they have done in the light of the principles of leadership.
VARIETY	Case studies, indoors and outdoors exercises, small group discussions, plenary sessions, lectures on key points, films or videos, and individual checklists all create variety. Keep them guessing what is coming next.
ENJOYABLE	The enjoyability of a course is important, because if it isn't enjoyable adults will learn but little. But if it's *only* enjoyable that's tantamount to failure.
RELEVANT	If neither the participants nor the trainer can see any relevance to the actual job of leading or managing that they are doing, or shortly will be doing, it's unlikely the course will be effective.
SHORT	About two to three days is right for most leadership courses at all levels. Beyond that the programme is in danger of becoming repetitive or academic.

This list is not exhaustive. Good leadership training, for example, should also be EVALUATED and it should also be REPRODUCIBLE if you want line managers or their equivalents to be the leadership trainers, as at Sandhurst.

Each of these principles can be debated at some length. The brevity or conciseness of the leadership course outlined above caused much comment. The reason for the shortness of the functional leadership course at Sandhurst was, however, that the whole two year programme was conceived as a leadership development course, in keeping with the basic purpose of Sandhurst. Skills training in leadership functions, as I have explained, could be pursued symbiotically with tactical training in the field. In recent years the idea of short courses within an overall in-company programme, which includes both on-the-job training and open learning opportunities for individuals, has come to appeal to industry and commerce. It is now long courses which need justification.

LEVELS OF LEADERSHIP

Leadership exists on different levels. The work I have described at Sandhurst applies to developing leadership for what might be called the first level: leadership of the primary small group in the organization, ranging from about five to twenty-five people (the functional leadership course is also used for training non-commissioned officers in the armed services).

The second or middle level of leadership is a broad band. Its characteristic is that the leader has more than one group or team, each with its leader, working under his direction. (One doctoral student of mine named it *ambient* leadership, a word taken from the Latin verb for walking about.) In so far as an infantry platoon has three or four sections, each under a non-commissioned officer, the platoon commander is verging on this wide middle band of leadership, which stretches up to the top.

Strategic leadership, as it has been called, describes the next discernible level: leading an organization, such as an army, an industrial company, a university, diocese or large school. Above that level one enters the stratosphere of politics with national leadership – the grand strategy or policy of a nation – and then international leadership.

You may be thinking that this is a somewhat hierarchical way of looking at leadership. In so far as human society is intrinsically hierarchical I shall stand by that interpretation. But leadership is not to be confused with command, management, episcopacy or governance. There is an a-hierarchical, almost an anarchical strand in leadership which needs always to be borne in mind. Democracy, in the sense of the equal value of all men and women, and leadership go together hand-in-hand. For good leadership is the personal answer to the question, 'How do free and equal people combine to get things done?' Now democracy, the growing sense of spiritual and moral equality, stands at loggerheads with hierarchy on the emotional level. Perhaps hierarchies will only be acceptable if they can justify themselves and if they are well-led.

Alongside the hierarchical concept of leadership levels - leaders of tens, hundreds and thousands - we should therefore place a different framework. It starts in the same way - learning to lead others to achieve worthwhile tasks - but it grows in terms of quality and its highest level is a form of distinctively human leadership. That leadership - that spark which touches our power to transcend ourselves and *become* ourselves - can appear at any level of a hierarchical organization or completely outside the boundaries of hierarchy.

* * *

The basic principle of leadership training - that it is wrong to give a person any leadership role without some specific leadership training for it - is often accepted and applied at the bottom of organizational pyramids: it is less commonly applied to the middle level of leadership, and rarest of all to the senior or strategic level. There it is assumed that a senior manager or equivalent has the necessary powers of leadership in a developed form or else that leadership is no longer relevant. These assumptions will be examined in more detail in Part Two.

The hourglass model of career change which I have developed throws some more light on levels of leadership. Some people in organizations, I suggest, follow career paths that resemble an inverted funnel. They begin broad-based at school, then choose between Arts and Sciences (too soon in Britain, many argue), and then specialize still further. The process is repeated or continued at university and in postgraduate training, especially in the science-based and vocationally-orientated courses. Again the process is repeated or refined further when a person enters employment: he or she is - or will soon become - a specialist. In some organizations - IBM and the Civil Service are examples - it is possible for such a person to progress to the top, in terms of salary and status, while remaining essentially an individual contributor. It is a bad feature of British industry in the past - and parts of it today - that specialists such as engineers, scientists, accountants or salesmen can only be promoted by being made managers and put in charge of others. For many specialists such promotion is as unwelcome to them as it is unfair to those who must work for them.

For many other specialists, however, becoming a manager fits in with their career plans. Their potential for 'getting results through people' may have been evident to them for a long time, or it may have been first identified in the selection process of the organization in question. Whichever way, they *want* to be managers or leaders.

At that point in their careers they are moving through the narrow neck of the hourglass – it may have been long or short in their cases – and are becoming generalists again. The degree to which they will retain a specialist contribution to the output of the organization clearly varies from situation to situation. But the pattern has been altered: the new generalist role should set the tone.

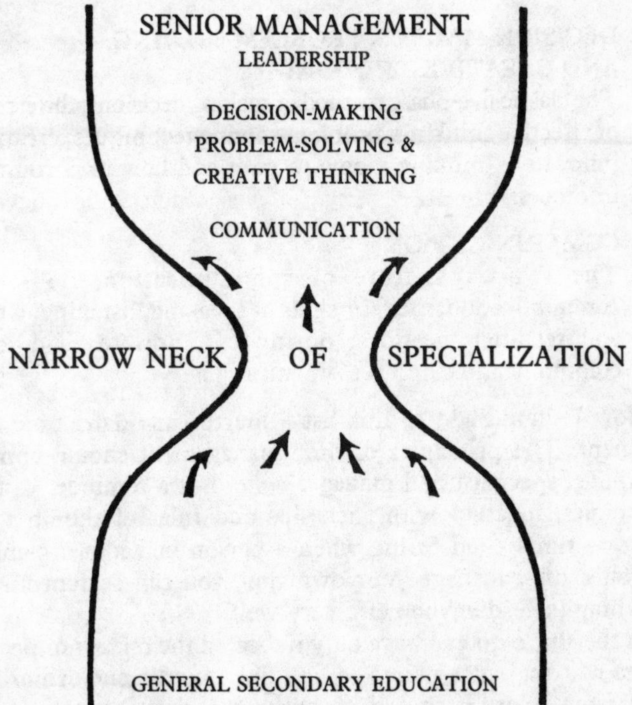

HOURGLASS MODEL OF CAREER CHANGE

Two 'widening' processes need to occur if a person emerging from the narrow neck is to advance eventually to a strategic leadership role. First, his or her knowledge of the enterprise as a whole – finance and marketing, production and distribution in the case of industry – needs to be developed and consolidated, partly by training but mainly by experience of managing or working in more than one area of the organization's operations (see the following chapter).

The second development, often neglected, is a growth of the understanding and competence in what Douglas McGregor called 'the human side of enterprise'. That embraces three core elements:

- LEADERSHIP
  Leadership in small groups – task, team and individual; leadership/management functions; the decision-making continuum; the principles of leadership development; leadership at different levels.

- DECISION-MAKING, PROBLEM-SOLVING AND CREATIVE THINKING
  The classic five-phase method of making decisions; the elements of effective thinking; problem-solving techniques; creative or innovative thinking – how to do it and how to encourage it in others.

- COMMUNICATION
  The two-way nature of communication; non-verbal communication; the four skills of speaking, listening, writing and reading; meetings; downwards, upwards and lateral communication in large organizations.

Now I should add to this list a fourth candidate: time management. The principles of time management should apply to everyone, specialist and manager alike. But a reminder of those principles, together with such tips and rules of thumb which exist, is timely and fitting when a person becomes a manager. If you cannot manage your own time you can seldom manage anything or lead anyone else very well.

In the above notes I have only indicated the *content* of possible courses at the entry-points to first-line, middle and senior level leadership roles. It should go without saying that the *methods* employed should reflect the principles or hallmarks of leadership training listed above. The level and age of those involved in courses will affect the methods employed. For example, outdoor leadership exercises are seldom appropriate for those about to be made field-marshals, archbishops or vice-chancellors: they belong to the first-line and to the lower-middle levels of management.

CONCLUSION

Too much emphasis on the word or even the concept of leadership and leadership training can be counter-productive. The attributes of a good leader and a good follower overlap. That is fortunate, because most of us are leaders, subordinates and colleagues. If it is done properly, leadership training should be a gateway to the 'transferable personal skills' required to perform all three roles with excellence.

Is training in the shape of courses out-of-date? Will it be replaced by individuals using open learning systems? Although I shall argue later that open or distance learning programmes, including computers and interactive video, do have an important part to play they should never be seen as replacements for well-run leadership training courses. For leadership is about people. Leaders need to be trained with people: in groups for effective leadership – or membership – of teams at work. Remove people and you reduce leadership training to a mere ghost of its former self, without form or substance.

The British have been world-leaders in devising methods of leadership selection and leadership training. The steps forward in this field over the past quarter century, as recorded here, have done a great deal to transform managers into leaders. But there are still many more organizations that could benefit from introducing such courses, especially as part of a general strategy for leadership and management development.

KEYPOINTS

- Courses in leadership — formal or informal training — constitutes only a small part in the formation of a leader. But it is important to get this training element right.
- The path to successful courses lies in the seven hallmarks: simple, practical, participative, variety, enjoyable, relevant and short.
- The sovereign principle is to keep it simple. That doesn't mean being simplistic or superficial. As Einstein once said, 'Everything should be made as simple as possible, but not more simple.'
- Leadership training, like leadership itself, should be fun. There is no excuse for being boring or dull about what is, after all, one of the most fascinating and mysterious subjects in the world.
- According to the well-known 'Peter Principle', leaders are often promoted to the level of their incompetence. That may be the result of a faulty or inadequate internal promotion system. Or it may be because your organization has failed to provide these leaders with an opportunity to stand back, reflect and review again the principles of leadership in the context of what lies immediately ahead.
- Good leadership training also equips people to be more effective in the other two principal roles in organizations: subordinate and colleague, or — if you prefer it — team member.
- Leadership is learnt principally by experience and practice. Ideas and principles can help to prepare people for leadership roles and to cut down the time and/or cost of learning on the job. Courses are the best way of introducing those principles in a way that influences subsequent performance.

You cannot teach a man leadership — you
can only help him to find it within himself.

4 A Career Development Policy

These leaders were like trout swimming against swift currents. They couldn't stop ... indeed, they sought the advancing currents; they sought change. They had an upstream orientation ... these men could be characterized by a sense of restless dissatisfaction.

In order to reach the top and become a main board director or chief executive (or their equivalents) the potential of a manager as both leader and manager needs to be recognized and developed. A major way of doing that in large organizations is through career development. Its governing principle is simple:

Give the right job to the right person at the right time in order to develop his or her abilities — for the benefit of both the organization and the individual.

In practice, of course, it is seldom easy to apply that principle. For that reason many directors and chief executives are appointed who lack sufficient width of experience or depth of background. They have not been really tested and proved in a range of management jobs, some of which have called for outstanding powers of leadership. It is important that those responsible for leadership development should consider introducing at least a modicum of career planning into their organizations, if they have not done so already.

ON CAREERS

Career is now used so frequently to describe a person's progress in life, or, by derivation from this, his or her profession or vocation, that it's difficult to recall that it once meant a racecourse and a gallop — hence the phrase 'careering about'.

The origin of *career* is the Latin word for carriage road. It came to be used for racecourse, gallop, and by extension any rapid and unrestrained activity. It came to be applied first to the advancement of diplomats and politicians, and then to indicate progress in a vocation, and finally the vocation itself. Nowadays it is used about all jobs which have some implicit promise of progress, but most widely for jobs with explicit internal development — 'a career in the Civil Service'. *Career* now usually suggests continuity if not necessarily promotion or advancement.

The distinction between a *career* and a *job* only partly depends upon this implication of progress and development, for it is associated also with some class distinctions between different sorts of work. Does a carpenter or a miner have a career or job? The extension of the term, as in 'careers advice', somewhat dilutes these associations, but they cling on obstinately in the form of hidden assumptions. The same class undertones cast their long shadow on the distinction between 'development' and 'training' — the former is thought fitting to managers and the latter held to be suitable for use about workers or young people. In fact it is usually managers who need training while everyone else needs development!

It is interesting that the early use of *career* carried a derogatory sense of being unrestrained in one's progress upwards or onwards. That is still present in the words *careerism* and *careerist* — one who advances his or her career often at the cost of integrity.

Another derogatory note is struck when people refer to their career as a *rat-race*, by which they mean they experience it as a violent, senseless and usually competitive activity or rush. It is a phrase that vividly recalls the original metaphor of the racecourse. Perhaps managerial careers become rat-races for their owners if there is no training, no planning, and no sense of purpose.

The very concept of a career suggests that there is some explicit internal development, some progress or advancement. It is natural that those who embark upon a career should want to move up the ladder as high as they can. That doesn't imply that they are all careerists, although you will always find a few in every walk of life. The steps on the ladder are promotions to bigger and more important jobs, usually signposted as such by the salary that goes with them. In the context of developing leadership, each significant step will normally involve a larger responsibility for people. It should also take you onto the higher and steeper slopes, where the challenge of leadership is greatest: the risks of failure are more awesome and the rewards of success are correspondingly greater.

The more that people share decisions which affect their working life the more motivated they are to carry them out. It would be foolish not to apply that principle in the field of career development.

Granted that an organization or an industry (in the widest sense) has able people who are keen to have a career when it comes to steps on the ladder — or even choices between ladders — then it needs to work out a system to ensure that people come up to the senior roles of operational and strategic leadership with the right experience and training behind them. How does an organization do that?

SUCCESSION PLANNING

There are two basic approaches to career development. One starts with the person and works forward. The other starts with the senior leadership roles and works backwards.

One essential system in most organizations, especially the larger ones, is *succession planning*. Beside each job, especially in the senior management, three or four names of probable, possible or potential successors should be written down.

If the present job-holder suddenly resigned through ill-health who would succeed him or her? That name is the *probable* successor.

The *possible* successors should include one or two names of younger managers. Bear in mind that one recent survey of 200 chief executives revealed that the average age when they entered senior management was thirty-two years. They achieved the top job at an average age of forty-one. On the way up these 'high-flyers' had worked in eight or more different jobs in two or three different organizations. Behind these facts we can glimpse an essential story, admittedly speeded-up in the case of budding chief executives but true for all who aspire to rise as leaders in organizations. It is the process by which a specialist becomes a generalist by planned career moves.

A CASE STUDY OF CAREER DEVELOPMENT

Devona International is a large conglomerate, consisting of 980 companies organized into nine divisions. They operate in 36 different countries, making and selling a range of consumer products. The group is owned by an American, Dutch and British consortium.

All employees are divided into twenty-four salary categories, and each is rated annually as an A, B, C or D performer in their category. There are also four development lists, and senior managers are asked to place the names of their subordinates on one of those lists by identifying what they might be doing in five years' time. This discipline forces out vague phrases such as 'I think he's a high-flyer.'

There is an annual planning cycle in each company, accompanied by a personnel management meeting. This is attended by the chief executive of that business and his personnel manager, and the divisional chief executive and his personnel manager (who has a dotted line responsibility to the group personnel director at the centre). They discuss the progress of the top group of managers and vacancies coming up.

Each participant at this meeting has a short summary of the annual appraisals of the managers they are looking at, together with a statement of the individual's own preferences for how their careers should develop.

The names of potential 'high-flyers' among graduate entrants are starred in their third year with the group. Devona recognizes the need to clear a path of career development, rather than merely make life easy for them. The group's personnel department do so partly to ensure that these high-potential graduates are not bored or frustrated in jobs below their capacity and partly so they don't leave the group. It is also done to fit them for greater responsibility. 'We don't tell them their names are on the list — it makes it hard to remove them from it. They usually get to know. About half come off the list.'

The characteristically difficult task facing an organization like Devona International is persuading the divisions and companies to release managers in order that they might diversify their experience. The request for a move for a young manager invariably arrives when he or she is in the throes of a uniquely difficult product launch!

Organizations which have decentralized for sound commercial reasons may find more difficulty in arranging such cross-postings. If that is the case they may need to review their attitudes and systems. Alfred Sloan, a great president of General Motors, once wisely said that the central issue in organization is the relation of the parts to the whole. Getting the balance right is not easy. Like equiposing two scales, once the balance is more-or-less right what is needed is constant minor adjustments. Within the sum of things, postings or promotions with the career development needs of the group (whole), as opposed to the division or company (part) in mind, is a relatively small matter.

Just those company managing directors who are reluctant to release people may want someone in three or four years' time, possibly as a potential successor. 'I don't want him,' they will say of a suggested name, 'he has only worked in one place.'

Apart from the understandable reluctance of some parts to release people for work in other parts of the organization for the common good, there are other reasons why potential 'high-flyers' may turn down career development moves. Working wives or husbands who don't want to leave their jobs, children at school who shouldn't be moved at this stage of their education, and the need to be near an ageing parent, are but three of the reasons given.

In an international organization like Devona a refusal to work overseas will obviously limit a manager's career. The refusal to work in different parts of the country for a manager within a national organization will have the same effect.

CONCLUSION

If your organization is getting it right it will not allow the leaders of tomorrow to stagnate in jobs. That does not mean they should be moved every year before their mistakes have a chance to catch up on them! There has to be time to achieve some objectives, to build up a 'track record', but the emphasis should be upon onwards and upwards. That means wider knowledge, gained through working in a range of functional areas, on the staff as well as in line management. It may include secondments and periods away from the organization altogether. This widening of experience, however, should be coupled with a deepening of the manager's understanding of strategic leadership within competitive environments and eventually of industrial statesmanship with a changing world.

THE LADIES' HANDICAP

Even when the path is normally open — when there is nothing to prevent a woman from being a doctor, a lawyer, a Civil Servant — there are many phantoms and obstacles, I believe, looming in her way.

Virginia Woolf

KEYPOINTS

- It is essential for organizations — the chief executive and the principal staff person on the 'human resources' side — to draw up a succession plan for the more important jobs.
- The very word career implies progress or development within a work context. Leadership development in organizations should be integrated closely with the steps an individual takes upon the career ladder.
- Among the names under each job in the succession plan there should be at least one of a person in his or her twenties or early thirties.
- Large organizations lose one of their advantages if cross-postings for the purposes of management development cannot be made. The parts of a corporate body should never be allowed to become so particular that the interests of the whole are sacrificed on the altar of divisional profits.
- Drawing up succession options shows up vulnerable positions, opens minds to unusual possibilities and engenders a sense that succession is in control.
- Career moves should be aimed at developing general capability, not merely at grooming a person for a specific job.
- Involve people as far as possible in decision about their professional future.

The process of development which takes place in a company is rather like a steeplechase. As you jump over the various obstacles and challenges you build up your experience and stamina. Also the same race weeds out those who are unable to cope effectively.

5 Line Managers as Leadership Mentors

> *At a crisis in my youth, he taught me the wisdom of choice. To try and fail is at least to learn; to fail to try is to suffer the inestimable loss of what might have been.*
>
> *Chester Barnard*

In the development of a leader of stature one or more mentors have often played a significant part. What is a mentor?

The word *mentor* is derived from Greek mythology. When the hero Odysseus left Ithaca he entrusted his son Telemachus to an old friend on the island named Mentor. The goddess Athena took Mentor's shape on more than one occasion to help Telemachus in the difficulties that befell Ithaca during his father's absence. Under Mentor's inspired tutelage the untried youth eventually became a seasoned leader.

Telemachus appeared at first in the story as a good and dutiful son but lacking in spark or drive: he was timid and unenterprising. Later, at the behest of Athena working through Mentor, he ordered his mother's domineering suitors to depart. When they refused, guided by Mentor, he resolved to sail to the mainland and report the calamitous turn of events to his father. As the story continues Telemachus demonstrates ever more resolve, energy and resourcefulness. When Telemachus eventually joins Odysseus upon the latter's return to Ithaca, he acts as an intelligent and enterprising helper. He astonishes his mother Penelope, for example, by taking command in the house and leading the fight against the over-mighty suitors.

This Greek myth does illustrate a truth about leadership. Leaders are inspiring. In order to become so they need to be inspired themselves. Mentors are those who inspire us with a vision of leadership. They often do it as much by their example as by their words.

I sometimes think that leadership is like a torch handed from one runner in a relay race to another, rather than a subject which can be learnt from a book. It is a matter of the spirit. Some people — very few in my experience — have the power to ignite the fire by the sparks of their words or presence. They may be quite unconscious that they are acting as leadership mentors. Characteristically such mentors have a high opinion of you:

- They perceive more within you than you can see yourself.
- They encourage you to set demanding goals and aspire to high standards of conduct, both professional and personal.
- At times they seem to expect or require a great deal from you, more than you feel capable of delivering.
- But their example and their support proves to be decisive and you rise to meet the challenge.

CAN MENTORING BE DEVELOPED?

A review of my own experience makes me initially doubtful if mentoring — as it has been called — can ever be organized or systematized. It is the natural inclination of managers to turn everything into systems, as I have already suggested. It would be convenient and nice if everyone in a hierarchical organization was a mentor to the ten or twelve people who report to him or her. But it is not as simple as that. To send out a memo to all managers directing them to become 'leadership mentors' is unlikely to be effective.

Could line managers be trained to do so? A proliferation of courses in coaching, counselling and appraisal suggests they can.

Going back to the three circles, a part of the leadership strategy in all organizations should be to persuade all line managers that they own the third circle — *developing the individual*.

The levels at which they operate in that third area will vary considerably. On the swimming analogy, almost everyone can be taught to swim but few will ever reach the highest level of Olympic performance.

Line managers who are taking the three circles approach seriously will accept that developing the individual includes developing his or her leadership potential. That involves far more than just sending the person concerned on a course. It means trying to do 'on the job' leadership training. That involves the function of evaluation in the form of appraising the individual — identifying strengths and weaknesses, encouraging, advising and listening. An annual appraisal interview should be the annual stocktake. It is both the summation of all the informal reviews during the year and the time when the balance sheet of the year's performance is reviewed.

Before and after a person goes on a leadership course he or she should be briefed and debriefed by the person he or she reports to. The talk prior to the course is to establish clearly why the organization thinks it worth spending their money and his or her time on the course. The person's training needs and the course objectives have to tie up. Afterwards the line manager will want to know what the course member has identified as action points, so that he can help in implementing them. The course may have suggested changes in the way the department or section is organized or run, which will need digesting — sometimes with a strong drink!

If your line managers are themselves leaders of some stature, leading by example as well as precept, the young managers will be learning a great deal more from working with them, observing them and talking to them than they can ever put into words. If that is happening, they are well on their way to becoming leadership mentors.

To be realistic, however, some line managers plainly lack the necessary leadership qualities — not to mention the inspiration of Athena — to act as mentors in developing leaders.

One possibility is for the chief executive to appoint as mentors, or 'godfathers' and 'godmothers', some senior managers who do not have line responsibility for the young manager. Some organizations have followed this route with good effect, especially with graduate recruits.

Another possibility is to allow a young manager to choose his or her own mentor within the organization, not unlike selecting a father-confessor. This method works well in some contexts where hierarchy is not strong. For example, I know one head of a university department who decided to follow this course after attending a leadership course. Upon her return to the university she approached another head — a wise person — to act as her mentor in matters of leadership and management. Both have enjoyed and benefited from the relationship.

What are the qualities of a good mentor? Professional and personal integrity are essential. Wisdom is desirable. Wisdom is not the prerogative of the old — there is no fool like an old fool. A good mentor has natural teaching ability, which draws the best from you. If you have found a good mentor, then thank God — or Athena — for him or her.

POINTS FOR REFLECTION

The most valuable executive is one who is training someone to be a better man.

Robert G. Ingersol, 1883

There is a point with me in matters of any size when I must absolutely have encouragement as much as crops rain: afterwards I am independent.

Gerald Manley Hopkins

Correction does much, but encouragement does more. Encouragement after censure is as the sun after a shower.

Goethe

KEYPOINTS

- Most successful leaders can look back upon one or two persons who acted as leadership mentors in their careers. Such mentors are natural teachers. Being wise — intelligent, experienced and good — they can also act as counsellors or guides pointing out a path forwards in times of perplexity.
- All line managers are potential mentors. They can become active mentors by taking a personal interest in those that work for them. That means finding time to listen, to offer encouragement, to delegate, to coach if necessary, and to give some guidance if asked. If you do the spadework of mentoring in this way the chemistry of relationship will usually look after itself.
- Some managers are uninspired leaders because no one has ever taken the time to inspire them. Inspiration is contagious; leadership is caught as well as taught.
- The best mentors are the least conspicuous.
- Anyone who expects to join a top team should be able to prove that he has developed at least three people capable of doing his job.

We learn only from those we love.

Goethe

6 Research and Development Adviser

Research is cheap if you want to stay in business, expensive if you don't.

Any large organization or enterprise that means to develop its managers and leaders must have a staff specialist capacity — an individual or a group — with responsibility for keeping the chief executive and the senior leadership team up to date on how to grow managers and leaders.

That principle, I hasten to add, is not an invitation to follow the latest fad in management development. What is newer is not always what is truer.

But you should certainly have your antennae out in the fields of management development and leadership development. Keep your eye on what counts for best practice in organizations which are acknowledged to be successful over a relatively long period of time. If possible, visit these organizations and talk to their management development specialist. Attend seminars or conferences on a selective basis — if they promise to help you to keep up to date in the field.

The individual or committee charged with this responsibility must obviously do more than read books or attend conferences. I suggest three items for the agenda: training the trainers, course evaluation, and the importance of conducting experiments in leadership development.

TRAINING THE TRAINERS

From what has already been written about formal and informal leadership training, it will be clear that much depends upon the quality and training of leadership course trainer or tutor for this kind of work. The ideal trainer should possess natural ability and experience as a leader in his or her own sphere, a working knowledge of the general theory of leadership at a greater depth and width than the level on which he or she is expected to teach, and reasonable skill in a variety of educational methods. Few people possess all three qualifications in the same high degree. But although much of the creative work in designing training programmes may be done by two or more minds working together, committees do not make good teachers.

In the majority of cases the only practical solution is to choose as instructors men or women with the first type of experience and to add on to it some specialist training in the role of a leadership trainer. But a high order of ability as a leader is not a guarantee of success as a leadership trainer: the two roles are interrelated yet not identical. There will always be a small proportion of instructors who naturally perceive the distinction and adapt accordingly; a majority of the others may be trained for the job providing they possess enquiring minds which are open to new ideas and new ways of doing things without losing their critical faculties.

The degree of knowledge and experience in all three senses possessed by the prospective instructors is a key factor in determining the content and shape of the syllabus. By the provision of common written and visual material, and by the careful selection of educational methods, a minimum standard can be achieved throughout an organization's training programme. And so the employment of professionals in designing a course can dramatically mitigate the mistakes of a poor teacher (and, incidentally, give the new instructor the confidence of knowing that all does not rest on his shoulders). But above that minimum much depends upon the natural or acquired ability of the instructor, and the quality of the training made available to him will be a vital factor in deciding the level of his performance.

EVALUATION

Organizations which value manager-leaders tend to invest money in developing them in a variety of ways, notably by sending their managers and supervisors on internal and external courses. Someone should have the responsibility for auditing training in terms of its overall effectiveness. In the context of leadership courses, that means a critical assessment in terms of the five criteria identified on page 34.

It is a matter for some concern that as leadership and management courses have become widely accepted as part of the scene in industry and commerce so the emphasis of evaluation which marked the early days of leadership training in the 1960s has weakened. The failure of 'management science' and 'behavioural science' to come up with any 'scientific' measures of effectiveness, despite much time, money and effort, may partly explain this retreat. Management consultants of all shapes and sizes who have entered the field of leadership/management training cannot spare the time or money to evaluate their courses properly. The only evaluation that matters to some of them is repeat business.

If the academics cannot — and the purveyors of courses will not — carry out evaluation studies, organizations must do it for themselves. It is an imperative to do so, because one of the chief functions of leadership is evaluating or testing performance against standards. It can be done. If the teachers do not evaluate their own work how can they expect their students to review critically and objectively their team's and their own performance against objectives or standards?

EXPERIMENTS

If an organization never experiments in leadership training it will learn nothing. Moreover, the specialist staff in the leadership development field will be in danger of becoming mere office managers, paper-pushing bureaucrats or semi-academic theorists. All leadership training should remain experimental. A finished or perfect programme would be the end of the road. Within that grand experiment there is plenty of room for small experiments, subject to the obvious constraints of cost and time. 'Try it out, try it out,' says the wise chief executive, knowing that an experiment is usually better than committing the organization to a wholesale change or a massive new computer-aided system. The fact that the change or system which so excites the personnel department has worked in other organizations, even if they are in the same field, is not sufficient evidence that it will work in *this* organization.

* * *

One of the hardest things to do in any institution established to educate and train people in leadership is to maintain a balance between the interests of the staff and those of the students. The staff can sometimes forget that the models, ideas or examples that seem such 'old-hat' to them still come as blinding bolts of lightning or as the fresh dawn of insight to young people and, indeed, many not-so-young ones as well. Repetition can hardly be avoided in leadership training, but training should never be mechanical. The fact that the course participants are always different makes every course different, however similar the content. A careful watch should be kept for any distortions of content or erosions of training methods which can blight leadership training. These 'improvements' usually stem from a staff member's desire to add or subtract, alter or develop. Sometimes I get the impression that leadership courses I am asked to evaluate are being run more for the self-actualization needs of the staff than for the learning needs of the course members. It was once said about a certain young ladies finishing school that 'the pupils did not make much progress but the staff improved enormously'!

Of course there must be changes, both in content and method, but well-tried and tested models should not be abandoned until one is absolutely sure—supported by some consensus in the trade—that a better theory or a better method has been discovered. One gets lost gradually, by taking small but incremental steps away from the 'straight and narrow' of good, simple leadership training practice.

Experiments are essential both within a strategy of leadership development as a whole and within the content or methods of particular courses, programmes and systems. Mounting and monitoring these experiments — showing initiative and critically reviewing the results of one's initiative — should be on the agenda for the specialist person, committee or unit charged with advising on leadership/management development and training.

Research is an organized method for keeping yourself reasonably dissatisfied with what you have.

Charles F. Kettering

KEYPOINTS

- A specialist research and advisory person, supported by a group, is needed to keep the whole leadership development strategy under regular surveillance with the aim of improving the quality of explicit and implicit leadership education.
- Such a person or body is the natural focal point for training the trainers, evaluating courses and initiating experiments in personal and professional development.
- Such a person should be a professional in the field of leadership or management development, but he or she is unlikely to be effective in that role unless backed by direct experience of leading and managing in the relevant industry.
- Experiment is the lifeblood of research and development.
- Monitor leadership courses closely; for distortions of content can easily occur. Good training methods, based on principles only half-understood by the instructors, can also slide gradually into incoherence. Keep to the hallmarks.

> *The only way in which the growing need for leadership in management can be met is to find the potential leader and then start his training and give him the chance to lead.*
>
> *Field-Marshal Lord Slim*

7 Getting the Structure Right

Structure without life is dead. But life without structure is unseen.

John Cage

Every organization is like a building, a combination of the naturally connected and dependent parts of a whole. Structure refers to the manner of that putting together or construction of parts as well as the product of it. The word comes to us from a Latin verb meaning to build. It is especially useful for discussing the internal relations of organization. Its drawback comes from its early uses in building, engineering and science: it conveys something relatively fixed and permanent, even hard. But human enterprises are living processes. To borrow the language of physics, they are — or should be — *dynamic* structures as opposed to *static* ones. On the other hand, changing internal structure too often can cause confusion.

Structure should be as simple and clear as possible. It should be purpose-built in the sense that serves the particular nature of an organization by enabling it to fulfil its purpose with the minimum amount of resource wastage.

THE DECENTRALIZING TENDENCY

The chief executive of an organization is also its architect. On the building analogy, he or she has probably not designed the original organization. It may or may not have been purpose-built: some organizations grow like rambling old houses or unplanned villages, bits being added on here and there. The chief executive must consider whether or not the time has come for some architectural alteration of the house internally.

There are fashions in structuring organizations just as there are predominant styles in building or rebuilding. If the chief executive calls in professional organizational architects or interior designers (management consultants) they will usually recommend the fashionable style, which is to decentralize profit responsibility and functions from central headquarters to local 'profit centres'.

In the context of developing leaders that tendency has been undoubtedly beneficial. The operational managers in charge of the parts need to be leaders, entrepreneurs and businessmen. In the past they were often little more than ciphers, passing information upwards and instructions downwards. Now they are set free to lead: they have an independent command, subject only to some strategic and financial control from the centre.

In order to achieve proper decentralization it is necessary to eliminate unnecessary levels of organization. The levels which interpose between the centre and the 'profit centres' or their equivalents should be carefully scrutinized to see if they could be discarded. Many organizations are still over-managed and under-led. Two organizations with whom I have worked in recent years — ICI and British Rail — have both stripped out a whole layer of management.

The 'leaner and fitter' organizations which result from this kind of structural surgery help to develop leaders primarily because there are now opportunities for leadership. Opportunity acts like a magnet to managers who have leadership within them.

The group personnel manager of one large multinational bewailed to me the other day the loss of these extra tiers of management—especially such posts as deputies—in his own organization. He had opposed the change, arguing that deputyships were good development appointments. How far he was merely rationalizing I leave you to judge. Clearing the organizational jungle has certainly had the unfortunate effect of destroying the natural habitat of the Greater Spotted Managerial Bureaucrat, now on the danger list of threatened species.

SIZE OF GROUPS

A key factor in getting the structure right is to determine the optimum size of working groups. Various studies have suggested that the optimum size depends on such factors as the technology used by the group and the geographical spread of its members. There are no simple answers.

Another method is to start with the three circles. A leader or manager is responsible for the three circles: achieving the task, building the team and developing the individual. With how many people can this be done?

Individuals, for example, now should expect to discuss their work with their leader, possibly on a day-to-day basis. They require information, support and encouragement if they are going to do their jobs well.

A good leader will want a relationship to evolve between himself or herself and each member of the group or team, in addition to the primary relationship with the team as a whole. Each of these relationships will be different. That takes time.

SPAN OF CONTROL

Those who wish to disprove the validity of all principles of management usually start by criticizing the principle of span of management (or span of control). The principle is usually attributed to Sir Ian Hamilton, who never intended stating a universal principle (but rather was attempting to make a personal observation in a book of reflections on his army experience) when he said that he found it wise to limit his span to three to six subordinates.

No modern believer in general principles of management relies on this single observation, and indeed, few can or will state an absolute or universal numerical ceiling. Even Lyndall F. Urwick's often cited limit of six subordinates (a limit which is by no means accepted as universal) is hedged and modified by requirements of 'direct supervision' and 'interlocking operations' of subordinates; in fact, these conditions tend to make the numerical limit meaningless.

Taking the three circles fully into account suggests that no leader or manager should be *directly* responsible for the work of more than about twelve people. They are the ones with whom he or she will set objectives and review performance in some agreed way. These team members will have direct access for help or advice. Apart from providing encouragement and guidance in the short term, the manager in charge should work in partnership with those twelve or so people to develop their full potential for the future.

CONCLUSION

Structure in the context of leadership development really comes down to *opportunity*. A good structure creates opportunities for the exercise of genuine leadership in management; it doesn't stifle it by overloading leaders with too many people. Nor does it frustrate leaders by giving them accountability without the necessary authority to act.

Achieving the proper balance between the levels of management in the structure with the optimum size of high performance teams is a matter for judgement. Remember that the perfect constitution doesn't exist. Because your organizational arrangements will always be to some extent unsatisfactory — the shoe pinches or the harness chafes — you will always need good managers in order to achieve outstanding results *in spite of* the way they are organized.

Having said that, you should ask your managers on a regular basis: 'Are there any ways in which this organization could be better structured? How can each individual be enabled to contribute more fully to the common task?' Once you detect a consensus among the replies it is time to consider making some structural changes.

Keep an eye on the barometer of bureaucracy. Quintessential managers have a tendency to try to run things by impersonal, mechanistic systems. These internal systems usually involve a multiplying of rules, much form-filling and mounting paperwork. Once it gets a hold bureaucracy is self-generating and it multiplies profusely. In no time at all you will find your simple and clear structure obscured by the green ivy of bureaucracy growing indoors faster than your secretary's pot-plants. It wraps its tentacles around your leaders and drags them down to being no more than mere managers or administrators.

KEYPOINTS

- Structure should reflect the living processes of an organization.
- Be willing to alter structure inside an organization in response to external or internal change — radically if necessary — but do not do it too often. Not more than once in three years is a good guide for major changes. People need time to adjust to a new structure in order to work well in it. If you change too often it confuses them.
- Get the size of working groups right if you expect managers to become leaders in all three circles.
- Always listen for ideas on how the structure can be improved and implement the good ones right away.
- Cut out unnecessary paperwork and bureaucratic procedures — the 'treacle' which slows down movement forwards in organizations to a snail's pace.
- Organizations usually have a logic for their present internal structure; often it is implicit rather than explicit. Understand that logic before you import remodelling ideas from other kinds of organizations.

A good organization tends to simplicity.

Sir Arthur Helps

8 Self-Development

I am always ready to learn but I do not always like being taught.

Winston Churchill

'The ancient Japanese art of Bonsai uses subtle wiles and infinite pains to restrict the growth of a potentially mighty tree. Yet the same effect can be achieved on your career in management by quite the opposite process. By doing little or nothing. Which is why it is so important to take action. And to do it *before* the rot sets in.' So began an imaginative advertisement for a management course.

Can people develop their own capabilities or possibilities themselves? Clearly the answer is yes they can. Although we cannot entirely pull ourselves up by our bootstraps in any sphere we can contribute a great deal to the process of professional or personal growth. That principle applies to leadership. As Field-Marshal Lord Slim said, 'There is nobody who cannot vastly improve his powers of leadership by a little thought and practice.'

CHANGING ATTITUDES

Everything begins with attitudes. Some people are natural self-starters and self-developers. Others have to be sold the idea that they have real potential as leaders and that they 'own' the problem of developing that potential. Sometimes the benefits of such self-development in terms of career prospects have to be spelt out, just as parents do for children.

One obstacle to self-development, now much reduced, was the old belief that education ended at school or university. It might be capped by a period of further professional or technical training before one got on with the job. Elsewhere I named this assumption the Clockwork Mouse Theory: they wind you up in your youth and you gradually run down until retirement.

Fortunately there must be few managers or professional people who think like that now. If there are any left they have not heard the message of the times. The impact of social, technical and commercial change has developed a much keener awareness that education and training are processes that should continue throughout our lives. People are now much more disposed to the idea of self-development. That greater willingness to assess one's own strengths and weaknesses, and to embark upon programmes for improving one's skills, presents a considerable challenge to organizations if it is to be properly met.The National Westminster Bank was one of the first companies to embark upon leadership training along the lines I have been advocating. In 1987 it became the second UK company (after ICI) to break through the one billion pounds a year profit barrier. That year John Fricker, NatWest's controller of group training, outlined a shift of emphasis towards self-development in training.

NATIONAL WESTMINSTER BANK: A CASE STUDY

We need to recruit sufficient better people, retain a higher proportion of such people, and develop them for wider career and business needs faster than before. So, two years ago, we instituted a new management development programme.

Although this is not the only route to management in National Westminster, it lies at the core of our management development. It is geared to identifying future managerial talent and to providing relatively early training and development opportunities for recruits. In the past, we have tended to leave such opportunities until rather late in a person's career. In addition, we are trying to provide more opportunities for older staff with management potential.

The management development plan starts with a detailed selection process, involving psychometric tests, interviewing and other devices, leading to accelerated training for those accepted, zig zagging people through a variety of real jobs faster than they would otherwise experience. The plan is based on personal development training programmes, which take the trainee through three stages:

1. A self-development centre, which takes up one week at the bank's residential staff college and aims to provide insights

into the trainee's personal strengths and weaknesses and career aspirations. It is based on the principle of an assessment centre and examines leadership potential, problem solving ability, interpersonal skills and basic skills in oral and written communication. So far, 1,000 people have been through this stage.

2. Personal learning programmes, which last between six and 24 months, depending on the needs identified in stage one. These take place at work. Each person is provided with a personal development adviser — a mentor, counsellor and coach—and learns both on-the-job and through personal learning packs, self-paced open learning materials for use in the trainees' own time in the workplace. Once the trainees have reached a stage in this process where they are recommended for further assessment, they go to:

3. The career development centre, where a more realistic picture is assembled of a person's future abilities and likely career.

The programme was introduced only two years ago but 2,000 are already going through the system, with 300 so far having reached stage 3.

Organizations like the NatWest are following the logic of self- development by planning to provide more distance learning, particularly through computer-based training. As I have said already, in my opinion distance learning and computers have only a relatively small part to play in learning about leadership. The nature of the subject dictates that. Because it concerns people and their feelings it has to be learnt through living contact and involvement with other people.

SELF-DEVELOPMENT IN THE LEADERSHIP CONTEXT

How then does the principle of self-development apply? First, nine-tenths of self-development is motivation. You have to *want* to become a better leader.

Career ambition as a principal motive can be a spur to self-development, but it's not much use by itself if the potential for strategic leadership is lacking. Without the incentive of advancement, however distant or however ill-defined, few people will submit themselves to a proper programme of self-development as leaders. Shakespeare once called ambition 'the soldier's virtue'. Perhaps one of England's great soldiers, the Duke of Wellington, struck the right note when he wrote in a letter early in his career: 'I do not worry about promotion, it will surely come.'

Self-development in leadership boils down to one word: opportunity. A self-developer will find out what opportunities are available in the shape of internal or external courses. Proactiveness may be needed. You may have to suggest to your manager or the personnel manager that it would be a good thing for all concerned if you went on that course. Opportunity in the shape of the next job that will stretch you more as a leader is also a priority. Again you may have to be proactive in proposing yourself for a career development move. Wellington's gifts needed no advertising: those with more modest talents must manage their own public relations if they wish to climb the ladder!

EXPLOITING OPPORTUNITIES WHEN THEY OCCUR

Since so much in most careers is unpredictable the process of leadership development involves accepting challenges and seizing career opportunities as and when they present themselves. This characteristic is found in the biographies of all successful leaders. A potential leader should always be on the lookout for occasions which may be used for personal development. One recent survey of management development gave these two examples:

> 'I was running one of our major businesses when the managing director of an even more important one was accidentally killed in an air crash. I had the opportunity to take over his position. It was the first time I had independent total responsibility of this kind and it had a major impact on my development.'

'How was I chosen for my job as head of the group? I just happened to be there when the merger of our two companies occurred and I was offered the opportunity.'

Most chief executives think that the chief reason for their success is being in the right place at the right time, followed by hard work and acceptance of early responsibility.

For it is a fundamental axiom in leadership development that the person concerned 'owns' the problem of developing his or her leadership potential. The benefit for an organization in applying this principle is that it can enter into a partnership with its young leaders or leaders-to-be which is to their mutual advantage. The former can supply opportunities, training and encouragement, whereas the latter brings high motivation and the willingness to learn. Both have to be honest with each other in their relationship. In particular the organization must strive to give its honest impressions, in the form of realistic feedback, of how far up the ladder of promotion a person is likely to rise. Has he the makings of a strategic level leader? Those impressions may prove wrong, but they should be given.

The apparent disadvantage of such a policy, of course, is that the manager concerned may come to place his self-development as a leader in front of the needs of the organization, but this drawback does not stand up to serious examination. But the organization and the individual concerned may agree that a further opportunity within the organization is lacking, and so it makes sense to look elsewhere. Remember those 200 chief executives? On average they had worked for two or more organizations.

THE WILLINGNESS TO STUDY

Self-development involves the willingness to study. Although books are now supplemented by workbooks, audio and video tapes and interactive computer-based programmes, reading is still the core method of learning. As Francis Bacon put it more than three centuries ago: 'Reading maketh a full man; conference a ready man; and writing an exact man.' Fullness or completeness of character, readiness in discussion, and accuracy in the expression of his or her thoughts and purposes are surely important attributes for the leader. And they all depend on his education and perhaps more precisely on his self-education, the only education of permanent and lasting value. Bacon adds this excellent advice on how to read: 'Read not to contradict and confute, nor to believe and take for granted, nor to find talk and discourse, but to weigh and consider.'

> THE LEADERSHIP CHALLENGE
>
> Those who vow to do good should not expect people to clear the stones from their path on this account. They must expect the contrary: that others will roll great boulders down on them. Such obstacles can be overcome only by the kind of strength gained in the very struggle. Those who merely resent obstacles will waste whatever force they have.
>
> Albert Schweitzer

KEYPOINTS

- Self-help is essential for developing leaders. Organizations should encourage all their employees — not just the managers or leaders — to develop themselves as leaders and team members.
- Training courses in leadership are no more than opportunities for those who wish to learn. You cannot teach a person leadership — you can only help him to find it within himself.
- In order to develop oneself, theory or principles must be brought to bear upon one's practice or experience. Books and other distance learning methods have a part to play in that process.
- You cannot ride a bicycle until someone gives you a bicycle. Self-development is best done by doing the work of a leader, not thinking or reading about it. Action first, then reflection.
- Mentors — experienced leaders — can be an immense help to the young manager. Self-development includes seeking out these teachers and benefitting from what they have to say.
- Learning is a gradual process of absorbing, testing and retesting; you try something — it works in some circumstances, not others — you reflect.
- Leaders are seasoned by failure. Failure teaches success. If you are not making mistakes you are not trying hard enough.

> *Development is always self-development. Nothing could be more absurd than for an enterprise to assume responsibility for the development of a person.*
>
> *Peter Drucker*

9 Organizational Climate

> *Everyone knows at any given moment who is the best company in its field. Not necessarily in terms of size or profits, though it could be. I mean the best in bringing in new products, market sensitivity, presence, range, quality, how we deal with our people, ethical, environmental and safety standards — all of these things.*
>
> *Sir John Harvey-Jones*

In order to grow anything the climate has to be right. Leadership develops in a climate or atmosphere of trust, for example, while it withers in a climate of distrust, suspicion, and cynicism. Nor does authoritarianism, which leads directly to dependency, do anything to grow leadership.

Climate and culture can be linked together. The best-selling management book *In Search of Excellence*, by Tom Peters and Bob Waterman, has done much to put the phrase 'organizational culture' on the map. The authors did not say what they meant by culture: most writers on management or organizations don't either. As culture is one of the two or three most complicated words in the English language that is probably wise. In this context, however, I can offer you Aldous Huxley's definition:

> *Culture is the sum of special knowledge that accumulates in any large united family and is the common property of all its members.*

Knowledge in that definition needs some unpacking. It includes knowledge of 'the way we do things around here', as well as knowing the history of the group or institution — its myths and heroes, its triumphs and disasters. This history is seldom learnt from a book: it is handed down by oral tradition.

Writing about Sandhurst in 1968 I stressed the perennial importance, as far as the development of leadership goes, of the general ethos of the place and the people who made up the Royal Military Academy:

'Atmosphere, by its very nature, is difficult to analyse and almost impossible to convey to others. The pink-white building of Old College, guarded by those six gleaming brass guns taken at Waterloo, the Chapel lined with memorials to fallen officers, the traditional parades and ceremonies of the Academy: all these exercise their own pervasive influence. Moreover, careful attention has always been paid to the selection of those officers and NCOs who come to Sandhurst as instructors for three-year tours of duty. This means that officer cadets who, like all young people, are naturally and keenly observant, can learn much by seeing good examples in the course of their everyday military studies.'

When I came to identify the five ingredients of successful leadership development at Sandhurst (structure, leadership course, field leadership training, research and advisory staff, and staff training) I included this dimension of general ethos, climate or culture under the broad heading of structure.

THE IMPORTANCE OF VALUES

Writing about Sandhurst reminds me of one obvious point — so obvious that I do not think I was then even aware of it — the British Army *values* leadership. That high value was expressed in various ways, both explicit and implicit. The field-marshals of the day — Montgomery and Slim among them — came down and addressed the officer cadets and staff on leadership. At the Sovereign's Parade in 1965 the Queen said some memorable words which summed up the message of Sandhurst:

'You have learnt here that an officer must be, above all else, a leader; a person whom men will follow into danger, discomfort and every ordeal which nature, climate or a human enemy can contrive. Remember always that the best and purest form of leadership is example; that "Come on" is a much better command than "Go on".

'You come of races renowned for courage and I know that as officers you will never fail to be the first in danger. But leadership in the stress and excitement of battle will not be your only responsibility. Your patience, inspiration and attention to detail will also be required in the often equally testing routine duties and in what may seem uneventful and even unimportant periods of service. These times call for leadership of a special kind if you are to keep the morale and efficiency of your men at the pitch required.

'Leadership demands a dedicated responsibility towards the men under your command. Their lives will be in your hands and they will have the right to expect from you the highest standards of character, professional competence and integrity. If you will always put their interests and welfare before your own, you will not fail them and together you will be able to undertake any enterprise.

'You will often inspect your men, I suspect that when you are doing so they will be just as keenly inspecting you....

'The path on which you are now setting out will often be rough and steep; my trust, my thoughts and my good wishes go with you on it.'

Not all the armed forces of other countries place such a high value on leadership as the British Army, the Royal Navy and the Royal Air Force have traditionally done. Something of that ethos has rubbed off on other armies which British officers have raised, trained or led. In the Arab Legion, for example, in which I served, Glubb Pasha had inscribed on the inner courtyard wall of each of our Jordanian desert forts:

Example is stronger than orders. Improve the morals of the people by your own good example.

When Glubb visited units he often initiated a discussion among the officers on the importance of leadership by example.

Because leadership was part of the culture, men like Lieutenant-General Sir John Glubb and Lord Slim, when there was no formal leadership training course at Sandhurst in their day, grew into fine leaders. The whole structure and ethos centred on leadership.

Turning to industry, commerce and the public services, when I began to work in those areas in the late 1960s, it became swiftly evident that the cultures of the constituent organizations placed no such high value on leadership. Indeed they sometimes regarded leadership as an essentially military concept, alien to their own purpose and sub-culture.

The reasons for this original state of affairs and the changes that have transformed the scene are complex and mainly historical, so I shall omit them. Now there are a growing number of industrial and commercial organizations, schools, universities and other public services, who are coming to value leadership in management — and in the work force — in ways that influence young people entering them for the first time as well as that all — important person — the customer.

THE SECRET INGREDIENT

In the 1930s a Japanese naval officer cadet on a course at the Royal Britannia Naval College at Dartmouth was found by the orderly officer wandering around the corridors late at night with a notebook in hand.

'What are you doing?' he was asked.

'I am looking for the lectures on leadership,' replied the Japanese cadet. 'Obviously you give these lectures in the middle of the night so that we students from foreign countries should not be privileged to attend and learn about this subject which is so important to you.'

KEYPOINTS

- Culture, ethos and climate are words that point to an intangible but highly important dimension of leadership development. Culture means the way of living, thinking and feeling of a group of people following a common set of values.
- A common knowledge or tradition about leaders and what they do is a core ingredient in organizational cultures in which leaders grow.
- Such organizations have one characteristic in common: they place a high value on leadership in command or management and insist upon its presence.
- Example is contagious, be it good or bad. An organization with a high proportion of good leaders — and leaders for good — will develop a climate conducive to nurturing leadership.
- Other important elements in organizational climate include a proper delegation of authority. It stems from a warmth of relations and a mutual trust between levels of management based in turn upon mutual perception of professional competence and personal integrity.
- Leaders are there to create a positive atmosphere in organizations, so that they can achieve their tasks. Morale describes a group or organization's attitude to its work.
- Changing an organization's culture when necessary is one of the supreme challenges for a strategic leader.

Ultimately, it is our values that give us the stars by which we navigate ourselves through life.

Sidney Simon

10 The Chief Executive

> *I believe that the principal reason why some firms survive, prosper and expand, while others dwindle, perish or sell out, must be sought in the personalities of the men who manage them.*
>
> *Charles Wilson*

By chief executive in this context I mean the leader of the organization or institution, be he or she known as chief executive, chairman, managing director, vice-chancellor, president, vice-president, director-general, bishop, general, minister or any other of the traditional titles given to the person who is ultimately in charge.

I have already made the assumption that senior roles of this kind are essentially leadership roles. That does not mean, of course, that the tenants of such roles are leaders or even perceive that leadership is required of them. The opposite is patently true in many cases.

There are two errors to avoid in thinking about the strategic leader or director-in-chief of an organization. The first error is to exaggerate the importance of that one person. Some people believe that if only they can find a hero in shining armour, a 'man on the white horse', to lead them, salvation will follow as surely as day follows night. In political life the world has seen this doctrine carried to its extremes this century in the horrors of fascism: *Der Führer* and *Il Duce* were the German and Italian phrases for 'The Leader'.

The other error is to go to the opposite end of the pole and dispense with a single leader at the top altogether. This usually means rule by a committee or an oligarchy of some kind. That solution can work quite well if things are running smoothly. But change, especially in the form of crisis, throws up the need for swift decisions and leadership from one person.

The truth lies between these extremes. All does not depend on the leader. The quality of the senior group of leaders — the leadership team — around him or her, the degree of leadership throughout the organization, or nation, the people themselves — their characteristics, education and training, attitudes, spirit and morale — and the technology, wealth and natural resources at their disposal, all these factors will help to determine the eventual outcome. Hannibal and the elephants of Carthage could not overcome Rome, nor could Lee and his Confederates vanquish the Northern States, though both Hannibal and Lee were the finest leaders of their day.

Equally, an organization which lacks good leadership at the top carries a heavy handicap in the competitive race. Rome's great strength and resources gave it time to find a leader in Scipio Africanus who could eventually beat Carthage. The Northern States of America, under the inspiring leadership of Abraham Lincoln, also had time on their side — after much trial-and-error Lincoln eventually found his general in Grant.

To summarize: large organizations and institutions, like nations, are led by a team of people. But that leadership team itself needs a leader, a *primus inter pares* or first among equals, just as an orchestra needs a conductor.

THE RISE OF THE CHIEF EXECUTIVE

In times of crisis, as history shows many times, free and democratic peoples tend to entrust power to one person to see them through. The exercise of that power is usually limited in extent by law and in duration. When the crisis was over republics such as Rome expected their dictators to emulate the worthy Cincinnatus, who resigned his dictatorship after the sixteen days during which he had vanquished the foe and then returned to his farm beyond the Tiber.

The economic recession of recent years produced much the same tendency in industry and commerce to strengthen the positional power of the person at the top, so as to free him or her to make the necessary decision, to cut out the dead wood and to provide firm, tough but fair leadership in the right direction. The new title, *chief executive*, reflected this shift of emphasis.

Executive is an American word for manager. It makes explicit the essential nature of a manager (as opposed to a leader or director), as one who carries out or executes policies or directives of others. Significantly an executive officer in the armed forces of the United States is the officer who is second-in-command. The executive branch of government in America is the branch responsible for carrying out the policies agreed by Senate and Congress. In business language, then, an executive is any person who holds a position of administrative or managerial responsibility.

In Britain it became common for a board of directors to appoint a general manager to supervise the work of other managers running the business. In the course of time the powers of the general manager were extended beyond supervision. As some senior managers became executive directors on the board, the general manager changed his title to managing director.

A former director-general of the British Institute of Directors, Jan Hildreth, noted the growing use of the chief executive title:

> 'If there is a distinction between the role of the managing director and the chief executive — and I believe there is — it is one of the degree of leadership required from each.
>
> 'The managing director must run the show from his position as an equal among his fellow board members. The chief executive must lead both the board and the organization; this includes running the people who are running the show.
>
> 'In essence, the chief executive represents a fine compromise between the need of any human organization for a recognizable leader, and the needs of the parties interested in an enterprise for a committee to protect and balance their interests.
>
> 'To succeed, or even to survive, in this most difficult of roles requires of the chief executive good health, humour, a resilience not given to many, and the powers of persuasion and personal leadership needed in both boardroom and workshop.'

Incidentally, the title of director-general was another import into Britain during the 1970s. It is the French equivalent to chief executive.

THE CHIEF EXECUTIVE'S CONTRIBUTION TO LEADERSHIP DEVELOPMENT

The principle of organizational climate or culture has already raised the importance of corporate values in leadership development. If an institution, organization or enterprise *values* leadership then leaders will come forward and flourish.

Of course there are other values which characterize successful organizations: excellence of product and quality of service are examples. Sometimes these values are captured in company slogans for the purpose of communicating them internally or externally as part of the public relations exercise. These pithy slogans are the modern equivalents of school or college mottoes, with the advantage — or disadvantage — that they can be changed from year to year. An organization which prizes its integrity will also have developed a code of ethics, which may be written or unwritten.

The chief executive plays a vital part in the organization's affirmation or reaffirmation of its core values. Within that spectrum falls the value placed upon leadership in management. Here the chief executive can contribute by talking about the nature and practice of good leadership, and by making time to visit any courses in that area which are being run.

When did you last hear the word leadership on the lips of your chief executive? If it is merely a fashion among the management developers in the company — their 'flavour of the month' — then leadership can be easily disregarded. It is when senior line managers who have acquired high repute talk about something as being important that younger managers or their equivalents sit up and take notice. Verbosity about leadership, half-digested snippets from books or articles, pieces written by assistants or — even worse — the public relations department, do not meet this requirement. Whatever the chief executive says should be simple, clear, vivid and based upon his or her own convictions and experience. Very little has to be said, but it has to be well said and repeated often in different words.

Some chief executives make the fatal assumption that by definition they must be leaders because they are chief executives. To restate an earlier point: you can be appointed a chief executive, but you are not a leader until your appointment is ratified in the minds and hearts of everyone in the organization — *everyone* — not just your fellow directors or the management as a whole.

Nobody expects top leaders to be perfect in terms of personal qualities, professional knowledge — so they never make mistakes — or in performance of key leadership functions. In fact great leaders are often great in both their strengths and their faults. It follows that lesser leaders also have their contradictions.

Groups or organizations allow for the realities of human nature and they give an 'idiosyncrasy credit' to their leaders. Providing you score enough marks in the task, team and individual circles your human frailties will be tolerated. Good team members will complement your skills and cover up your deficiencies. Perfection is not part of the job description, but people will respond well if they sense that you are leading to the best of your ability.

Visits to courses for developing leadership and teamwork within the organization ought to come high on the list of priorities for a chief executive. Apart from providing an opportunity to underline the message of the course and its relevance to the organization within a rapidly changing world, such occasions allow the chief executive to talk about the strategic thrust of the business and listen to the reactions of a cross-section of managers or employers. Taking people into your counsel — showing them the cards — is a powerful way of motivating them. Your presence confers recognition both on the subject and upon the actual or potential contributions of those present.

> *Example is not the main thing in influencing others — it is the only thing.*
>
> *Albert Schweitzer*

KEYPOINTS

- Organizational effectiveness benefits greatly from good leadership at the top but it is not wholly dependent upon it.
- Greater power and influence is accorded to chief executives or their equivalents, but there are also greater expectations of leadership focussed upon them.
- Leaders of very large organizations can do no more than set the broad strategy, create the right climate and develop the managers needed for today — and tomorrow.
- Chief executives can influence positively the growth of leadership at all levels by their words, their example and their presence in the training context.
- If the chief executive does not take action to develop leadership at boardroom level — and one step below — no one else will.

As the chief man of the city is, so will the people be.

Ecclesiastes

CHECKLIST: DOES YOUR ORGANIZATION DEVELOP LEADERS?

	Yes	No
Do you have a clear strategy for building good human relations that includes developing leadership at every level?	☐	☐
When selecting people for management jobs do you assess them in terms of their functional ability (task, team and individual) and the associated qualities of personality and character?	☐	☐

Are appointed leaders given a minimum of two days of leadership training?

Always ☐ Sometimes ☐ Never ☐

	Yes	No
Do you have some system for career development, so that future senior leaders broaden their experience and knowledge?	☐	☐
Are all line managers convinced that they are the real leadership trainers, however effective they are in that role?	☐	☐
Is there a specialist 'research and development' team who are keeping the organization and its line managers up to date–and up to the mark?	☐	☐
Has your organizational structure been evolved with good leadership in mind?	☐	☐
Do leaders, actual or potential, realize that they are the ones who 'own' the problem of self-development?	☐	☐

In the light of Chapter Nine would you say that there was room for improving the organizational ethos?

A great deal ☐ Some ☐ None ☐

Are your top man and his key team really behind leadership development?

Whole-hearted ☐ Half-hearted ☐ Not yet ☐

PART TWO *Some Developments in Leadership Training*

1 Functional Leadership Training Today in the Armed Services

Ten good soldiers wisely led will beat a hundred without a head.

Euripides

In 1969, when I left Sandhurst to become Assistant Director of the Industrial Society and form its Leadership Department, the functional leadership course was firmly established at the Royal Military Academy. Some twenty years later the three circles and the functional approach are still being taught at Sandhurst.

In the intervening years I have had comparatively little to do personally with leadership training at Sandhurst, or within the armed services as a whole for that matter. For five or six years in the 1970s I gave an annual lecture at the Staff College in Camberley — next door to Sandhurst — on the subject of leadership training, as I did also at the Royal Air Force Staff College at Bracknell and the Royal Navy's equivalent at Greenwich. But I have been kept in touch with developments.

THE ARMY

The long drawn-out emergency in Northern Ireland and the Falklands campaign have both provided plenty of tests for military leadership, especially at junior levels. The commander in the Falklands, Major-General Sir Jeremy Moore, was company commander at Sandhurst during the 1960s and taught functional leadership there. When Jeremy Moore left Sandhurst to become the commanding officer of the Royal Marine Commando Officer Training School he introduced the new leadership course there.

Without someone like myself present to act in the research and advisory function (the sixth principle) there must always be a concern that standards might slip or that necessary maintenance — on the analogy of a course to an aircraft engine — will not be carried out. For example, I saw a leadership brief for instructors at Sandhurst with the three circles drawn in a distorted way — with the team and individual circles in no contact whatsoever. This kind of thing can easily happen (see, for instance, Charles Handy, *Understanding Organizations*, Penguin, third edition 1987) and it can be as easily corrected.

Staff training is a case in point. Although the general system of staff training at Sandhurst serves well enough, it was always my view that *some* specific training for the trainers would pay dividends. Therefore I accepted with alacrity an invitation from the Commandant to conduct a leadership 'training the trainer' day for all the officers and some civilian lecturers of the staff at Sandhurst in September 1981. As the officers concerned were being recalled a day early from their leave I looked forward to the seminar as a challenge!

The aim of the day was defined by the Commandant as 'to refresh the old and indoctrinate the new on putting across the subject of leadership to officer cadets and student officers.' The day included syndicate discussions, a full lecture by me on the qualities, situational and functional approaches, and some skills sessions in observation, debriefing and counselling. The 'Mast Contract', an exercise using Lego bricks, was used by all ten syndicates in one of the sessions.

An evaluation form was issued at the end of the day and completed by 77 officers and lecturers.

The first question was 'As far as interest and relevance to your future work at Sandhurst are concerned how do you rate this day as a whole?' The result was that 56 officers rated the day between 'Excellent' and 'Good', with 20 grading it between 'Average' and 'Fair'. A number of useful suggestions were made later about improving the afternoon (which had dealt more with appraisal and counselling techniques than leadership training as such).

When asked 'to describe three ways in which you can improve your effectiveness as a leadership trainer' 23 respondents identified the need for more practice and experience, 12 wanted a standard observation form, and 10 thought the Sandhurst course should be longer.

'What would you like to know more about? What would you like to see covered at greater depth?' asked the third question. There was a very firm request (33) for more instruction on assessment, counselling and debriefing techniques. Some suggested the use of video to show good and bad examples which could form the basis for group discussion, and there was a feeling that more discussion on leadership methods was a necessity. Four officers requested more information about leadership techniques in industry.

The fourth question asked for specific suggestions on how Sandhurst as a whole could improve its leadership training. Suggestions included a course for new instructors when leadership is discussed in detail (9), greater standardization of doctrine at RMAS, more study days (5), creation of more command task opportunities in training (4), and establishment of a small 'research cell' in the field of leadership training (2).

To summarize: the overall feeling from the evaluation sheets was that the study day was a very useful exercise and of value to all who attended, because it encouraged discussion and ideas about leadership training techniques. The programme in the morning was considered very worthwhile but the afternoon programme (organized internally by the staff at Sandhurst) on appraisal and counselling skills could be greatly improved. More study days should be held to discuss, inform and teach the instructor body at Sandhurst about assessment, debriefing and counselling techniques. Lastly, there was a considerable feeling that new officer instructors should attend a short course on joining RMAS, when the content and methods in leadership training would be covered in detail.

For me this study day in 1981 confirmed a point that I had made with insufficient force in *Training for Leadership* (1968, pp. 74-75), namely that staff training is a key ingredient in effective leadership development.

* * *

On another occasion I was invited to visit a new development at Sandhurst—a company set up to take candidates who had narrowly failed to pass the Regular Commissions Board on grounds such as immaturity or lack of confidence. These candidates are given an intensive twelve week course in leadership, based on the functional approach. The results have been extremely successful. The company was named after Lord Rowallan, who established the first such leadership training unit for those who failed the War Office Selection Board in 1941. I was able to give the company commander copies of letters about that experiment which Lord Rowallan had written to me after the publication of *Training for Leadership* (1968).

In the wider context of the British Army an exceptionally thorough and systematic use of functional leadership, involving both a course and also field leadership training exercises, has been developed for the Territorial Army, University OTCs and the Army Cadets by Brigadier Michael Cawse (who in civilian life is Training and Development Adviser in DRG, the Bristol-based paper group).

THE ROYAL AIR FORCE

Readers of *Training for Leadership* (1968) will recall that the RAF Officer Training Unit at Henlow was one of the first to adopt the Sandhurst functional leadership course. When I visited Henlow I was most impressed by the professional way in which the leadership training was done. Neil Cameron, then Assistant Commandant at Cranwell (later Marshal of the Royal Air Force and Chief of the Defence Staff), organized a conference on leadership training at Cranwell at which I spoke; subsequently he invited me to lecture to the Royal United Services Institute, which I did in 1967 at a meeting chaired by the Commandant of Cranwell. After 1969 I had had no direct contact with the Royal Air Force except for my annual lectures at the RAF Staff College in Bracknell during the 1970s.

The Royal Air Force School of Education and Training Support at Newton has recently produced two valuable surveys of leadership training in the Royal Air Force. The first, by Squadron Leaders V. Hartley and M.R. Waring, is dated February 1985 and the authors kindly gave me a copy. The summary of the report states:

> 'It was found that most of the courses teach leadership as a series of theory lessons based upon Adair's 'Functional Approach' backed up by classroom and practical exercises. These courses have developed on an individual basis over the years to meet specific requirements. Most courses offer very limited pre-employment training in leadership to

their staff. Theoretical knowledge of the staff is not usually developed to exceed that contained in the course syllabus. There was sparse training provided in the practical skills of student assessment and debriefing, something which could adversely affect the training in leadership skills. However, there were exceptions to these norms...'

The second report, dated September 1986, set out to evaluate the leadership training element of the Initial Officer Training Course (IOTC) conducted at the Royal Air Force College, Cranwell. Again the author, Squadron Leader S.W. Tofts, gave me a copy. The summary reads:

'The evaluation did not seek to question the principles of Adair's Functional Approach to Leadership Analysis upon which the IOTC is based. Rather, it used Adair's framework for a leadership training programme as a model against which the IOTC might be measured.

'The study revealed that the basic structure of Adair's programme could still be recognized in the IOTC. However, in a number of important areas the structure had become distorted with the result that the course was better able to assess a cadet's performance than to improve it.'

Added to the recommendations for redesigning the course and introducing better staff training at Cranwell, the author suggested that the establishment of a post within the Ministry of Defence responsible for research and for giving advice to all RAF units involved in leadership training should be considered.

A study undertaken in 1987 found that some pilots leaving the service gave the poor leadership shown by senior commanders as a reason. As it takes about £3 million of taxpayers' money to train each pilot it seems worthwhile to look at ways of improving leadership development for higher ranks in the Royal Air Force.

THE ROYAL NAVY

The Royal Navy Special Duties Officers School at Eastney was the first Royal Navy unit to adopt the functional leadership course from Sandhurst. I saw the first course myself in 1967. When this school was merged with Dartmouth it took the course with them apparently, and the Britannia Royal Naval College adopted it from them. Apart from the series of annual lectures I have mentioned at Greenwich, two seminars for senior officers at the Royal Navy School of Management in Portsmouth in 1974, and some talks to Royal Navy Auxiliary Fleet captains, I have had no other direct contacts with the Royal Navy.

In 1978 the Royal Navy produced a comprehensive internal review of its leadership training, using 'the five areas of leadership training' in *Training for Leadership* as the main touchstones, together with a sixth—self-development. 'Self-development is the cornerstone of development of leadership abilities, and when all is said and done, training can only assist this process,' stated the authors of a subsequent study in 1979 on how best to implement the conclusions of the review. 'It will be suggested that the Navy has weaknesses (as well as strengths) in all these areas. The key to remedying them, it will be argued, lies in the creation of an effective Leadership School — the research and advisory staff.'

The cornerstone of leadership training in the Royal Navy, the report continued, would be Action-Centred Leadership. Following the recommendation in *Training for Leadership* (see also p. 40) the Navy associated the concept of communication and decision-making with leadership in the core context. In 1979, it was found, all leadership courses in the Navy were already formally based on ACL. 'There is, however, a varying degree of understanding and emphasis on ACL.' In order to set standards in leadership training and development, to train the trainers and to monitor and evaluate new developments, the formation of a 'lead school' in leadership at H.M.S. *Excellent* was proposed.

The Royal Navy did subsequently close its School of Management at Portsmouth. It also established a Royal Navy Leadership School at H.M.S. *Royal Arthur* at Corsham in Wiltshire. The primary purpose of the school, however, seems to be to train ratings in leadership to fit them for their future roles in the Royal Navy. The school also undertakes leadership training for officers and occasionally for representatives from the Fire Service and other civilian organizations. I do not know whether or not it, or some other establishment with a similar name, performs the job as specified so clearly in 'The Leadership Training Implementation Study: A Report on the Implementation of the Proposals of the paper "An Outline Approach to Leadership Training in the Royal Navy" (1979).'

THE FIRE SERVICE, POLICE FORCE AND PRISON SERVICE

Mention has been made of the Fire Service. Officers from the Fire Service Staff College at Moreton-in-the-Marsh visited Sandhurst in 1965 or 1966 and adopted the functional leadership course for their own use. Many hundreds of students pass through that college each year, and so it soon became a major user of the course. Visiting Moreton-in-the Marsh some twenty years later, in order to talk to the staff about leadership training, I found that the three circles was still taught but distortion had crept in to the content, the method had become watered down and there was a lack of staff training.

The Police Staff College at Bramshill, where I first lectured on leadership in the 1960s, has introduced with my help a leadership training course in the mid 1980s, run initially by tutors from the Industrial Society. I can remember contributing some sessions on leadership several years running to the Kent Police Force in the 1970s, but I have had no other contacts with training in the Police Force other than in recent years at Bramshill. Is there a strategy for developing leadership in the Police Force?

In 1968 the Inspector-General of Prisons invited me to participate in his conference for prison governors, and later that year I spoke at the Assistant Governors' conference. The seeds sown on those occasions have borne fruit, in that the three circles and functional leadership is now used as the foundation of the training of all prison staff. In 1988 I led two one-day seminars for all the senior staff of the south-east region, the largest region of the Prison Service.

CONCLUSION

It must be reassuring for all users of the three circles and the functional approach to leadership (*alias* Action-Centred Leadership) that the three Services still retain and evidently value this approach after more than twenty years of trial and experience. It is difficult to find examples of other leadership or teamwork courses that have proved themselves by that test in industry or commerce.

In 1968 I expected functional leadership to last for no more than about five years before something better emerged. But nothing superior to it has surfaced. American research (there is virtually none in Britain) has indeed thrown up plenty of novel theories to fuel some large international conferences on purely academic aspects of the subject of leadership (some of them funded by NATO), but nothing in the field of leadership training to rival the functional approach.

Extending a course beyond a 'normal life', however intrinsically durable it is, means it must be serviced and maintained with care in order to remain a coherent, effective and fresh course. A small research and advisory capacity, together with some provision for training the trainers (of trainers), is needed for all the uniformed services. In the 1980s I corresponded with two Chiefs of the Defence Staff to suggest that a joint conference between the Services on leadership training should be held, but my proposal was not taken up on grounds of expense. Nor could I subsequently persuade the Royal United Services Institute to do the job.

Without inter-service conferences on leadership training or research and development activities or advanced staff training, not too much must be expected from the functional approach in the Services. At least it has escaped academicization (to coin a new and horrible word) and it has remained remarkably cost effective. It still does a useful job within the strategies for leadership development pursued — explicitly or implicitly — by the three armed Services.

One clear area of weakness which emerges from various reports is the lack of any specific leadership training beyond a certain rank. (I am not counting the odd lecture on leadership given at staff college level.) The need to give brigadiers and above (or their equivalents in the Royal Navy and Royal Air Force) some oppurtunity over a day or two to review and revise their concepts of leadership, in the light of both their changing levels of responsibility and the circumstances of the day, does stand out clearly.

The three armed services in Britain are exceptionally good at growing leaders. In addition, they have been the pioneers in functional leadership training. With considerable generosity they have shared their experience of it widely. They must be regarded as the world leaders in leadership training. To sum up, leadership development in the armed services is very good, but in some respects it could be better.

Better an army of stags led by a lion than
an army of lions led by a stag.

English proverb

2 Admiral Sir Richard Clayton's Address on Leadership

It is upon the Navy, under the good providence of God, that the wealth, safety and strength of the Kingdom do chiefly depend.

Oliver Cromwell

Admiral Sir Richard Clayton played a major part in the extension of ACL to the Royal Navy. After beginning his career as a midshipman on destroyers in the Second World War he rose to become Commander-in-Chief Naval Home Command (1979-81) where he exerted considerable personal influence on the Navy's approach to leadership development.

The story goes that at a luncheon in Nelson's cabin on HMS *Victory* one of the guests, Lord Weinstock, was so impressed by what Admiral Clayton had to say about developing leaders in the Royal Navy that he invited him to join GEC with responsibility for management development, an offer which he accepted.

In November 1984 both Admiral Clayton and I were among those invited to speak at a national conference on leadership, organized by the Society for Strategic and Long Term Planning at the Royal Society of Arts. Tragically, a week before, Admiral Clayton was killed in an accident upon his motorbike. Admiral Sir Raymond Lygo, chairman of British Aerospace, who took his place, prefaced his own talk on leadership with these remarks:

> 'I am very sorry to have to be here today. The only reason I am is because my good and dear friend Dick Clayton is dead. Were it not so you would have had the privilege of listening to a man who spent a lifetime in the business of leadership and management in the Services and then brought that wisdom to bear for all too short a period in industry. Kind and considerate, rational and well balanced, he and I

used to talk from time to time about the problems of management and very briefly, because very few of us look back too much, at the differences we had found between the Navy and industry and of the differences we had experienced in making a transit from a Service life into industry. When I read Dick's notes for the speech he was going to give you today, I was struck by the honest straightforward simplicity of his message and of his emphasis throughout of the importance of the regimental system, of the importance of building morale, and of the importance of example. He based many of his examples on Arthur Bryant's book *The Rifle Brigade*, which illustrates how in a period of great pomposity and over-weening ignorance a new brigade was formed which broke with many hitherto accepted truths. It barely seems possible now, does it, that for many years in the British Army it was assumed that a title automatically bestowed qualities of leadership. The greater the title, the greater the genius. That led to disasters in the Crimea described in *The Reason Why*.

'Dick's example and his tolerance will long be remembered by his friends and especially by me.'

Sir Raymond Lygo then read some extracts from the draft of Dick Clayton's address as a prelude to his own thoughts on the subject. As a fitting memorial to Admiral Sir Richard Clayton, a great contributor to leadership development in the Navy and in industry, I publish below the full text of Dick Clayton's address.

★ ★ ★

LEADERSHIP IN THE ARMED SERVICES

When, several months ago, I was invited to speak at this conference on 'Leadership in the Armed Services', I accepted in that comfortable feeling of euphoria that distance always lends to such engagements — like the summer holiday prospect of an early-morning dip in the sea, so inviting the night before but increasingly cold and bleak the closer one gets to the water and to the moment of actually entering it.

However, even all those months ago I had some qualms. The very fact of appearing to be willing to stand up and talk on such a subject before an audience such as this — and especially under the critical eye of John Adair whose disciple I am and who knows more about the subject than I shall ever do — implies a conceit that I assure you I do not feel. I really am genuinely humble about leadership. I make no pretence always to have successfully practised what I so often preach. Even in what I preach, I make no pretence of being anything but a continual learner. I probably learnt more about leadership in my last two years in the Navy, when I was trying to define what I meant by it and how we could get people to do it better, than in all the other forty years. I am closely connected with leadership training in GEC and attend all our courses; and I never do so without picking up some new slant, or thought or perception. And the more I learn the more I realize how incomplete my perceptions and skills still are, and how difficult it is consistently to put one's theories into practice.

But having said that I *am* humble about leadership, let me also go on readily to admit that of course we in the armed forces *ought* to be *sensibly* humble about it because it is so essential to our effectiveness. There are indeed some writers and historians who have suggested that we have got a lot to be humble about; and whilst that, as a generality, would be very unfair — certainly when one thinks of some recent and current events, for example, the daily achievements in Northern Ireland, and our successes in the Falklands — I always remind my naval audiences that the history of mutiny in the Royal Navy shows how sadly often we have got our leadership wrong — and for every case where a failure of leadership results in actual indiscipline, there must be many others that result only in discontent, unhappiness, low morale, and poor achievement. The same thing must of course apply to leadership in other environments, but if our successes in the Services are more apparent, so can our failures be more dramatic. And the reason for that is that the need is so fundamental. Leadership is the one ingredient that the Services *cannot* do without.

* * *

What do I *mean* by 'leadership' in the Services? I run immediately into a semantic difficulty because of the limited vocabulary available to describe the range of ideas and concepts that I have in mind, and there is confusion and disagreement even about those words that are available. For example, if we were to ask a group of people from different backgrounds to define the difference between leadership and management we would probably get as many different answers as people. Some would make leadership the servant of management — others the other way round — and yet others might see little difference between the two. Furthermore, the limited vocabulary and our different uses of it make it especially difficult to differentiate between the levels at which the various skills have to operate — between at the one end the individual soldier and his section leader on the ground, and at the other the Commander-in-Chief miles away in his headquarters.

So since an arid debate about semantics will get us nowhere, let me make it clear that what I am after are the skills, perceptions, and attributes that are going to get the job done — appropriate to whatever level it may happen to be — and I don't mind if you call that leadership or management or a mixture of the two. I, personally, tend to use management more for the more mechanistic and academic skills, and leadership more for the inspirational and motivational ones. And whilst that doesn't alter my belief that *both* are needed in any true definition of leadership, and whilst, indeed, both are included in John Adair's three circles, this bias from my own Service background probably reflects a fairly universal difference of approach between the armed forces and industry. Though both pay lip service to the need for both types of skill, the armed forces tend to give greater emphasis to the motivational/inspirational skills, and industry vice versa. And though this emphasis can, and sadly often does, lead to some neglect of the other skills, it stems from the fact that the aims of each organization are fundamentally different.

The officers and men of the armed forces are, first and foremost, members of a fighting organization, and as General Hackett pointed out in his 1961 Lees-Knowle lectures, there is an unlimited liability clause in every military man's contract. He may be required to die; and he may have to die in loneliness and defeat and despair. Even in victory, some will have to die to help achieve it. As Field-Marshal Lord Wavell once wrote: 'The end of all military training, and the deciding factor in battle is that, sooner or later, Private So-and-So must of his own free will advance to his front in face of the enemy.' What sort of leadership is needed to achieve that?

I would like to break this down into three different aspects:

- *Leadership in Action* — the sort of inspired leadership that can lift people to do the almost-impossible, things that they would never have thought themselves capable of — the sort of leadership that can turn defeat into victory.
- *Leadership by Remote Control* — the sort of leadership that can motivate and inspire other people to do all those things on their own — even when they are lonely, and afraid, and with nobody to sit in judgment on them other than themselves.
- *Leadership in Training and Preparation and the Day-to-Day Routine* — the preparation of the soil within which the other two aspects of leadership must grow and from which they will take their strength. And because this is so fundamental, I am going to take it first.

* * *

Service in the armed forces is demanding — even in periods when not in action — indeed in a perverse and different way, sometimes especially when not in action. For example, I suspect that in the months that followed the end of actual fighting in the Falklands, the captains of all those ships that still had to go flogging around the South Atlantic — just in case they were needed — had just as much need to deploy sustaining and morale-boosting leadership as when the fighting was on. The Serviceman is often required to live and work in confined and uncomfortable conditions, and to accept (often without warning) long periods of separation from his family. At the same time he must be kept trained and prepared to the highest pitch so that if war does come — usually unexpectedly — he can meet the demands that will be made on him, demands that we and he may have been able to anticipate in kind but which will almost always be unusual and unexpected in precise form. All this calls for very special skills in leadership.

Of course over the centuries we have developed special cultures and systems to assist us. For a start, the armed forces have a strictly formalized hierarchical structure. This ensures the delegation and spreading of the leadership task throughout the structure; and it both assists and requires the development of leadership at every level. Our disciplinary code is designed to help us too. Whilst no society can exist without a disciplinary code, since it provides the communal framework within which we can all give of our best, knowing not only our own limits but those of others, the profession of arms demands generally a stricter framework than may be necessary in other societies because the pressures on the individual can be so extreme and the consequences of failure so serious.

But let me instantly dispose of the myth, believed by some, that in the Services we can rely on our various Discipline Acts to do it all for us. Inspiring and motivating people to give of their best, rather than instilling fear of the consequences, must always be a first and principal approach to discipline; and any breakdown of discipline, however small, implies a failure of leadership somewhere in the system. History demonstrates most conclusively that the most effective military units are those that develop and depend upon self-discipline, which means bringing forth the best in people and evoking in them the loyalty and sense of responsibility to live of their own free will within the established rules of conduct.

* * *

Perhaps the most important aid to good leadership and self-discipline in the Services is the way in which we organize ourselves into comparatively small fighting tribes, many of which perpetuate themselves as cohesive family units over the centuries and which are thus able to build up an ethos and a tradition that set the standards for all who belong to them. A good example is the British regiment of which Sir Arthur Bryant once wrote 'where is so much human achievement and virtue as in the annals of a British regiment of the line? Here is triumph over toil, monotony, discomfort, hardship and adversity; here is constancy and loyalty; here is heroism, self-sacrifice and devotion. And when a great regiment salutes its colours it is expressing this truth. Its members are commemorating their predecessors who suffered, endured and died in its service, and are dedicating themselves to do likewise.'

But even all that is only an aid to good leadership — not a substitute — and indeed without good leadership at every level, the regimental system can even have dangers. What, then, is the sort of leadership that is needed during this period that I have described as one of 'Training, Preparation and the Day-to-Day Routine'?

* * *

I cannot do better than start with John Adair and his three circles, which seem to me to contain all the essential ingredients of what a leader has to *do* in any circumstances. Of course, as in any other walk of life, precisely what is needed to satisfy the needs of the Task, the Team and the Individual will vary with the circumstances and with the level at which each leader is operating; and it is important to appreciate that in order to satisfy all those needs in a Service environment, military leaders will often have both to display in themselves and to develop in their subordinates those special virtues that are required by the profession of arms. Many of these — such as, for example, courage, fortitude, self-sufficiency, resource, loyalty, initiative, and readiness to 'have a go' may be important in any walk of life. But as General Hackett has rightly pointed out, they are imperative in the profession of arms because a force in which they have been highly developed will often be able to defeat in battle a stronger force in which they haven't. Now I appreciate that I am verging on the disputable ground of arguing what a military leader has to *be* is more important than what he has to *do*. But I suggest that in fact there is no real conflict here, since whilst what the leader *does* is certainly crucial, people in the armed forces need more from their leaders than the mere conscientious application of talent and method. Character also is indispensable in building up the essential climate of confidence and respect between leader and led, and in meeting the latter's needs when the chips are down and his life may be on the line.

This takes me from leadership in the day-to-day routine to my other two aspects of leadership where it has to succeed in the stresses and strains and demands of war. And of course there is a clear linkage between these two, since effective leadership in preparation, training, and the daily routine sets the foundations and lays the bricks of the structure of self-discipline and morale that helps us to effective leadership in battle.

* * *

What I have called 'Leadership by Remote Control' is clearly very relevant to the Army since soldiers may have to fight in very small isolated groups or even as isolated individuals. It is less obviously relevant to the Navy. Certainly when I stand on my bridge at sea and say 'Full Speed Ahead', the rest of the ship's company come with me, whether they like it or not. But even here, success or failure in action may depend upon individuals isolated within the ship. Successful 'Leadership by Remote Control' depends heavily, of course, upon all the work that has been put into preparation and training.

Only three points perhaps need special emphasis. The first is the personal example of the absent leader. The led will usually set their standards by his even when he isn't there — often even when he is dead. The second is the importance of people accepting personal responsibility for getting the job done at every level in the structure. Curiously enough it never occurred to me when I was serving that 'acceptance of responsibility' was a fundamental attribute of leadership. I suppose I took it for granted. It is only since I have been in industry that I have found it necessary to identify and emphasize it. But even within the Services some units are better than others at understanding and insisting on it; and some nations are better than others.

It is said that in Korea, the Turkish prisoners of war were the one race upon whom their Chinese captors were unable to make any impact and from whom they could not gain a single defector — largely, so I understand, because when the Chinese removed any Turkish leader — at any level — the next in line automatically assumed that role with all the responsibility that went with it.

Finally, the success of remote control leadership is wholly dependent upon trust — and upon trust in both directions. The leader will not achieve this unless, once again, he is perceived by his people to meet the needs of the three circles in ways that are appropriate to the circumstances — ways that may often be unconventional and wholly inappropriate to more normal circumstances. I don't imagine, for example, that General Orde Wingate was a terribly agreeable man, or that his leadership would be much fun to serve under in routine conditions; but it certainly seems to have met the needs of his Chindits in the jungle.

* * *

Which brings me to the third of my three aspects of leadership in the Services — 'Leadership in Action'. What the led will be looking for in their leaders in these circumstances, and what any action task will require (so, in parenthesis, both of these relate straight back to the three circles) are:

- Personal example — especially in the courage that any action situation is likely to require.
- Professional knowledge and the self-confidence that goes with it.
- An unhesitating acceptance of responsibility and the decisiveness that will go with that.
- An offensive spirit — and by that I don't mean that the leader has to be what some of my military friends call a 'cemetery man' (i.e. someone who leads you over the top and straight into the divisional cemetery) — but that he must have the determination and will to dominate his situation, rather than be dominated by it.
- And finally, that elusive thing called 'power of command' which in some ways is an amalgam of the other things I have just mentioned, but which includes also the ability to communicate effectively with crisp and clear commands.

All these things are 'doing' things rather than 'being' things, and they can all be developed in people and learned by them. It is thus one of the principal tasks of the armed forces in peacetime to develop these skills and attributes in their leaders at every level. So having tried to simplify my task today with the artificial if hopefully helpful device of considering leadership in the Services in three separate compartments, it must I am sure be evident to you that in practice they are all one. I emphasized earlier my contention that leadership in the daily round sets the foundations and lays the bricks of the structure of self-discipline and morale that helps us to effective leadership in battle, and to reinforce my own views on how I think it *ought* to be, though sadly not always how it is, I would like to quote a few extracts from Sir Arthur Bryant's *The Rifle Brigade*. [Here Admiral Clayton would have read out several extracts from the book, taken from pp. 23, 32, 166-7, 443, and finally, 160.]

That last quotation reflects the very strong sense of laughter and adventure, and the complete absence of dullness, earnestness and pomposity that runs through this history. Sadly, I can't claim that it is always like that in the armed forces — I wish it was — but it does, I think, make the point that leadership does not have to be goody-goody and dull to be effective — in fact quite the reverse in a military environment where the needs of task, team and individual can often best be met — sometimes, only be met — with a bit of robustness, panache, iconoclasm, and even eccentricity. This is very much a matter of personal style.

Years ago a friend of mine went out for a night dive in Malta with the Mediterranean Clearance Diving Team led by a tough old Chief Petty Officer. They took a 3-ton truck down to one of the creeks and when unloading it a young sailor said to the Chief, 'Chuck me down my flippers, Chief.' The Chief picked them up and threw them as far away into the gathering dusk as he could and said, 'Pick the f.....s up yourself.' Now the at-first-sight curious thing is that that sailor did not resent it at all. He laughed — and made a joke about it to his chums. That was how he expected a tough diving Chief to behave, and being treated in that robust way by an already established leader who had long before developed his own self-confident and very personal style did not in any way undermine the young man's basic self-respect. On the contrary, in that tough company it helped to make him feel a man among men and an accepted member of the team. So military leadership may often be more successful for being neither mealy-mouthed nor dull. But John Adair's three-circle doctrine still applies, and of course military leadership — like any other form of leadership — must adapt its methods to suit its personalities and the circumstances in which they find themselves. *I* could not have got away with how that Chief behaved, and not many officers could (though *some* might). As I frequently remind Naval audiences, the style of leadership that is necessary when fighting a boiler-room fire would produce poor results in chairing a meeting, and would rapidly lose one performers if trying to organize a ship's concert party.

* * *

Now I have been talking quite a lot about style, and I have also been arguing that character is important in a military leader. I have even been bold enough to identify certain attributes that I believe should form a part of the character and pattern of behaviour of this leader. All this aggravates the risk that I mentioned earlier that I shall be thought to be supporting a qualities approach to leadership rather than a functional one. But I have also suggested that in a Service environment that distinction can be a bit too black and white. I am not looking for characteristics that can only be inherited. All the character attributes I have mentioned can be acquired, although I admit that the Services' selection procedures do try to exclude those who are not thought to have the basic aptitude to acquire them easily. And the attributes are needed to able to carry out the functional task — i.e. meeting the needs of task, team and individual. Nor, of course, am I suggesting that we should try to force everyone into a completely common mould; we must all make the best use of those characteristics that we *have* inherited and not worry too much about those that we haven't.

But there are certain common things that the leader in the Services can and should aim for. In talking to young officers about this, I often use the analogy of Kipling's 'ship that found herself' in his short story of that name. This tells of a brand-new well-found ship setting out on her maiden voyage. She meets her first storm, and all her separate bits — the beams and stringers and plates and rivets — start chattering and talking to each other. To begin with there is argument about who is the most important and who is doing the most work. But slowly the bits bed in and start to work together; and as they do so, the individual voices disappear, to be replaced by the single strong voice of the ship – the ship that has found herself. I believe that something of the same sort happens with the development of the young leader. The bits are a mixture of his personal characteristics and those other attributes that we try to help him acquire. The sea is the military environment and the traditions of his Service and unit with which he is surrounded; and the storm – if you like – the sometimes painful experiences he will have to go through. If any aspirant to leadership in the services works hard enough at the bits and pieces, they will eventually blend with his inherited characteristics to create a style which, whilst meeting the common needs of the Service environment, will still be individual to himself.

* * *

There is one final and rather difficult facet to leadership in the Services that I have left until last. It applies especially in those circumstances where people are under the most strain. This is the question of Faith. Now although many great military leaders have found a firm religious faith to be a valuable support and guidance in achieving successful leadership and in demonstrating the moral values that are the basis of any stable and civilized society, and although when the chips are down most of us turn instinctively to God for help and comfort, I am *not* saying that a recognized religious faith is essential to a military leader. That could be disproved by a look at the history books. But I am sure that all of us need a belief in something, whether it be our God, our work, the society we are employed to defend, the regiment or unit we belong to or even ourselves. But it is a belief in something more important and more immortal than himself that will give the military leader a will to succeed and a kind of serenity in stress and danger that will communicate itself to those that he leads and will sustain their own determination and their own beliefs. This, again, is something that we have to encourage in our people, because men so motivated really can do the apparently impossible.

3 Outdoor Leadership Training for Managers

Without adventure civilization is in full decay.

A. N. Whitehead

One of the distinctive features of the last decade has been the burgeoning of outdoor leadership training for managers. I am frequently asked to give an opinion on the merits of such training and I usually answer by listing the various pros and cons of this approach. Here I shall add a sketch of the later evolution of this form of training (for its origins, see Appendix B).

Outdoor exercises of the planks and barrels type formed an integral part of the functional leadership course at Sandhurst. In my first experiment in applying the course to managers (in the builders Wates Ltd, 1966), the same outdoor exercises were used on a convenient building site adjacent to the head office.

When I joined the Industrial Society in 1969 it was more difficult to find places close at hand in London in which to do outdoor leadership exercises. I remember using the mews behind Robert Hyde House on the first ACL courses, much to the astonishment of the local residents!

The ACL training advisers in the Leadership Department almost mutinied at the prospect of carrying planks and drums around the country! The celebrated 'Mast Contract' exercise and various other exercises — which came to be known as table-top exercises — were developed in order to obviate this difficulty.

Some of the early users of ACL did not have that constraint and retained the use of outdoor exercises. In *Action-Centred Leadership* (1973) I reported that the Staff Training Department in the John Lewis Partnership was among them, despite the location of the firm in London's busy Oxford Street.

> 'The Planks and Drums exercise is used on fine days! We perform this on the roof of our building. It is particularly good for highlighting the contrasting attitudes of men and women at work. The nature of the equipment tends to bring this out — males doing the lifting and carrying and females experiencing frustration by what they perceive as suppression from the male workers. This is most evident in the feedback discussion phase and it can easily be related to on-the-job situations.'

It could be argued, however, that there was really not much difference between the indoor and outdoor exercises of the type I have been describing. The more extended use of the outdoors, more along the lines of field leadership training at Sandhurst, was a quite different concept.

"He's certainly demonstrated his leadership capabilities – he's got the whole lot of em on strike."

BACKGROUND

In 1966 one of my civilian lecturer colleagues at Sandhurst, a keen expedition leader, mentioned my work to Brian Ware, the

Principal of Brathay Hall in the Lake District, a centre originally established for providing development training for young people in industry. Brathay took on board the functional approach for its young people's courses in the next three or four years.

In the early 1970s the staff of Brathay and Peter Prior, then Group Managing Director of Bulmer, Britain's leading cider-makers, co-operated in designing and running an outdoor leadership training course for his managers. Peter was an unconventional person: pilot, diver and parachutist. He had a considerable enthusiasm for leadership, especially with a Services tinge — he had won the Croix de Guerre during the Second World War. In 1969 he recruited David Gilbert-Smith from the Army. David had commanded the Special Air Service Selection and Training Wing at Hereford, which was also the home of Bulmer.

The first Bulmer course led by David took place at Brathay in May 1971. Twenty-five managers of the firm took part. 'When we saw the programme,' wrote Denis Freeman, then Warden of Brathay, 'we wondered whether it was too tough. Bulmer must be a remarkable company — there wasn't a single failure.' The company's magazine devoted most of an edition to a fully illustrated account of the course, mixing humour with sound appraisement: 'One thing I failed to learn — how to make up a bed on a top bunk. It calls for some system of remote control,' and 'Comradeship, unselfishness, charity — old-fashioned words it is true — but in Brathay's setting, they ring still more true.'

The flavour of these early courses was captured by a reporter from the *Sunday Telegraph* in May 1972:

> 'Considering that their day began at 7 a.m. with a run, a game of volley-ball, and a round of the ropes-course, they are not looking too bad. But now these five businessmen and one police superintendent are in a bit of a predicament, marooned on an island in Windermere. "You've been washed up on a barren shoreline," says their instructor cheerfully, "there's the mainland, over there" he points to a rocky headland 60 yards away — "and there's your tackle. None of you can swim, and anyway the water's full of sharks. In 90 minutes there's going to be a tidal wave. So you'd better look lively."
>
> 'They set to. The tackle includes ropes, a pulley, a few sticks, two huge polythene bags, a bow and some arrows, and a light line.

Obvious beginning: to shoot a line-carrying arrow on the mainland...

'Elsewhere in the grounds of Brathay Hall, another group is struggling to heave its own members over a seven-foot electrified barbed-wire fence with strange affinities to the Berlin Wall. *Their* tackle — a few short poles, some string and a second, much bigger barrel — seems hopelessly inadequate; but according to David Gilbert-Smith, the wily ex-Special Air Service officer who devised the tests, the task is perfectly possible. A third group is in even worse difficulties trying to bridge a river.

"...and now let me explain our route in terms which you can best understand."

'The course is the invention of Mr Peter Prior, Group Managing Director of H.P. Bulmer, the Herefordshire cider-making firm.

'Two trial runs at Brathay Hall last year were so successful that they are being repeated and extended this summer, with the help and advice of the Industrial Society. Most of the "students" are executives from Bulmer aged between 25 and 50, but a leavening of outsiders is brought in. The central aim is to teach Action-

Centred Leadership, but the courses include a considerable amount of tough outdoor activity, such as mountaineering, rock-climbing and underwater swimming.

'"What I'm trying to do is to give people opportunities for achievement," says Mr Prior. "You may say — and plenty of people *do* say — 'What the hell has underwater swimming got to do with industry?' Well, I believe that learning some entirely new skill gives an individual new confidence, and that when he gets back, it brushes off on his work. I believe our experiment has opened up entirely new ground in management training."

'Already some other large companies have shown keen interest in a project of this kind. Whether they join in or not, it may be that Bulmer experiment will prove a shot-in-the-arm for adventure training as a whole'.

* * *

By 1973 Bulmer were beginning to run out of suitable managers for the course and so Peter Prior invited three or four other companies — all ACL users — to send groups of participants. I visited Brathay while this course was on and afterwards David Gilbert-Smith sent me the summary report on it, adding: 'Another enormous success as you can see despite the fact that as Chief Instructor I broke my elbow and dislocated my shoulder! A casual study of the findings places the physical practical outdoor projects way ahead of the academic theory sessions. I was most pleased with this course as we only had eight Bulmer candidates to 19 outsiders. In other words there was no captive audience. I think if you could find time to visit the next course you will be amazed at what the candidates themselves achieve and learn. It does very much prove the theory of ACL as a good fundamental basis to work off.'

In 1976, shortly after the Bulmer had hived off its leadership training activities into the Leadership Trust, David Gilbert-Smith wrote in a letter to me: 'As you probably know, we use your original concept as the datum point for our course learning. It is so simple, clear and concise, and as yet no one has come up with anything better.'

In 1979 the ties between the Leadership Trust and Bulmer were severed. The link with Brathay had already gone, for the Leadership Trust's courses were now run from a hotel in the Wye Valley. Ideas alien to ACL, drawn from the work of the

Tavistock Institute in London, were also added to the content of the programme. A harbinger of their shift of approach appeared in David Gilbert-Smith's booklet *Leadership in Management: Personal Leadership* (Leadership Trust, 1977), where he wrote:

> 'John Adair took a great stride forward in leadership thinking when he put together his concept of action-centred leadership identifying the three key areas of leadership: achieving the task, building a team and developing individuals. He also saw the relevance, balance and interrelationship of one to another. It proved a very useful model for guiding actions. However, on its own it does not take enough account of the human relations side, the interactions, personal qualities and changing pressures and circumstances. It is the personal leadership qualities of the leader which, in the end, will determine whether people will follow him or not.'

Whether or not my writings lend themselves to that interpretation I shall leave the reader to judge.

Meanwhile Brathay introduced its own series of 'Leadership for Managers' courses, which I helped to design. For five or six years I contributed to them with sessions on communication skills and decision-making, problem-solving and creative thinking (the ACL dimension being well covered by Brathay's Director of Studies and his staff).

Since the middle 1970s there has been a mushroom growth of centres and organizations specializing in providing outdoor training for managers. The extent to which they emphasize leadership varies considerably, for there has been a tendency to sell adventure training in terms of its general benefits to managers. Although I have some sympathy for this trend it does make even sharper the key issue of *transfer*. I hold no brief for this wider use of outdoors training for managers; here I shall restrict myself to discussing courses aimed specifically at developing or training leaders and team members which use the outdoors as a vehicle over a number of days.

THE PROBLEM OF TRANSFER

One of the main hallmarks of ACL, you will recall, is the

principle of relevance. At first sight a day learning to abseil down cliffs, or canoeing, or tramping through the rain on Britain's mountains, does not look relevant to being a manager in industry or commerce. The fact that managers may enjoy the experience is really neither here nor there: it would be unnatural not to enjoy a holiday in the mountains at the firm's expense.

People vary according to the width of their 'spans of relevance'. Some of us can see links between phenomena which to others seem totally unconnected. Others are allergic to any kind of analogy; for them all examples, case studies or experience have to be couched in the context and language of the industry in which they are working.

"Apparently it's no use shouting for help – course leader is in a meeting."

What I look for first in any course on leadership — indoors or outdoors — is the presence of models and principles which at least rival the ACL concepts. For it is the theory or ideas that will be transferred to the work place, not the outdoor activities.

Of course the model, theory, principle or generalizations can be reached by deductive methods directly from experience, but this takes a long time and it requires exceptionally skilled trainers. It could be disputed whether or not it is possible to have a purely deductive course in practice, though theoretically it is attractive. The best combination seems to be the introduction of some simple models and principles at an appropriate time in the programme, coupled with an alertness and sufficient knowledge on the part of the trainer to pick up other points which arise from practical work and to relate them to general principles. Leadership training works best with a mixture of deductive and inductive learning.

Transfer can be facilitated by discussion of application to the work place during and at the end of the course. I favour also the introduction of 'stepping stones', some exercises which help the students to bridge the gap between the functional leadership course and their actual roles as leaders, colleagues and subordinates. Field leadership training at Sandhurst really came into this category. The field training exercises were simulations of what a platoon commander would have to do in the field and the leadership teaching in the field served to reinforce the course's message and also to increase the likelihood of transfer after the officer cadet was commissioned and serving with his or her unit.

ASSESSMENT

Outdoor leadership training is more expensive in terms of time and money. The exercises or activities which are used as supplements or substitutes for the planks-and-drums or table-top type of exercises obviously take longer and they are often done — but not necessarily so — in residential centres or hotels in mountainous parts of the country. Is it worth it?

One argument for outdoor courses — that they create 'real tasks with real consequences' — is rather bogus. But it is certainly true that the tasks are often dramatic and highly enjoyable, and enjoyability is one of the hallmarks of ACL. The vivid memories created by them are important to learning, because vividness greatly helps recollection. For the man or woman who falls into a cold river because a bridge collapses, the value of planning is forever imprinted on the mind. It is difficult to create such powerful experiences in the classroom. Moreover, the outdoor course lends itself to more elaborate tasks, for example involving the leadership of geographically dispersed work teams.

The unfamiliarity of the environment and the tasks in relation to work have a number of advantages. It allows a clearer focus upon the leadership or management issues, unclouded by issues of business technology or professional practice. Its very unfamiliarity places all participants on an equal footing, bereft of the support or hindrance of hierarchical position or rank. People from very different backgrounds can be involved, which makes possible a fruitful cross-fertilization of experience and ideas.

There are less tangible benefits: the grandeur of the outdoors and the community fellowship which develops. A renewal of one's own values, coupled with a new personal sense of direction, can sometimes be among the beneficial outcomes.

Lastly, although I have said earlier that a potential drawback of this form of leadership training is the length and cost, it should be borne in mind that such courses create such a high level of involvement and energy that about 90 hours of work can be packed into a seven-day programme. Such an intensity of work could be a criticism but participants can cope with it in this context.

KEYPOINTS

- Outdoor or adventurous leadership training for managers is here to stay. The effectiveness of a particular programme depends upon how far it is based upon the well-established principles of leadership training.
- The extended use of the outdoors as a vehicle for training managers initially in the field of leadership training has led organizations to discover other advantages of this medium. The more general that training becomes, however, the more difficult it is to evaluate it.
- Look for the elements in the context of outdoor leadership courses — such as the three circles and the functions of leadership — which have a proven record for transferability. Check that the course providers are not letting the tail — the outdoor environment — wag the dog.
- Staff quality is an essential ingredient in success. As the staffs of outdoor development training centres often lack experience of leadership in management, it is a good idea to second them with managers drawn from your business as observers and co-tutors.
- The stimulus of uncertainty, which can be built into exercises in a natural environment, is especially useful in leadership training for middle managers.
- Leadership is about taking others with you on a journey. Leadership training done in the context of adventurous journeys can have a power to change people totally lacking in classroom sessions about academic theories of leadership.

I hear, I forget
I see, I remember
I do, I understand

ISINGTON MILL
ALTON
HAMPSHIRE

Tel: Bentley 3126

21-11-68

Dear Adair

I have just received your book on "Leadership". Thank you so much for sending it to me; I shall read it with the greatest interest.

Leadership is an immense subject. In 1961 I published a book entitled The Path to Leadership (Collins), in which I tried to show the way towards it. And in 1945 I gave a lecture at St. Andrew's University in Scotland on "Military Leadership".

Nowhere is it more important to teach it than at Sandhurst and in our universities; in fact to youth, since it falls on dead ground with the older generation.

Yrs sincerely
Montgomery of Alamein

4 Leaders for Tomorrow: The Universities' Contribution

A good beginning makes a good ending.

English proverb

Society has come to draw much more upon the ranks of university graduates for its leaders. That was always the case in the Church and the Civil Service. Now it is equally true of the armed services, industry and commerce. Leadership in the higher echelons of organizations increasingly calls for — among other things — intelligence and education, and a good university degree is taken to be some evidence for their presence.

As I shall show later, employers of graduates are looking for something more than evidence of good mental ability and subject knowledge. They are seeking what have been called 'transferable personal skills'. These include aptitudes for team work, if not leadership, as well as other attributes and qualities already mentioned in this book (also see pp. 134–5).

A DILEMMA FOR UNIVERSITIES

These requirements, however gently put, do pose a dilemma for universities which accept that they cannot be 'ivory towers' irresponsive to the needs of society, especially as society is now paying a major part of the bill.

One possible solution would be to leave the onus for developing transferable personal skills to employers. Against this line of thought I have argued that the years roughly between ages 18 and 21 or 22 are crucially important for identifying the values and big ideas that will exercise a major influence on our lives. Miss that boat and you run the risk that minds have been made up.

Secondly, I have pointed out that experience in the Services has demonstrated beyond doubt that it is possible to provide effective leadership training for young people (18-20 years of age) *before* they take up their first appointments in a command role.

There appears to be no real pressure from industry and commerce, it should be noted, to have business studies as an academic subject included in undergraduate programmes. Most major industrial or commercial employers of graduates are quite clear — and I agree with them — that they are the best people to teach management and business studies, subjects which anyway benefit by being post-experience. Not all employers, of course, do provide for such training, and many who do can be faulted for the way in which they go about it. But the post-experience years are really the time for studying the theory and practice of management and business. Prior to that, what employers of graduates are looking for with greater urgency are signs that universities are developing the whole person, not just the brain.

The dilemma of universities is that subjects are expanding rapidly and there is always pressure to do more engineering or medicine, for example. One expedient would be to lengthen university courses on the German model, but this could have a number of disadvantages from the angle of developing leaders. The sooner a potential leader gets out into the world and earns his or her living — and begins to learn from experience — the better. To prolong the years of academic study, even by tacking on slabs of management studies, would be a grave mistake.

THE UNIVERSITY OF SURREY EXPERIMENT

The solution, I believe, is to introduce a small ACL-type programme into the university syllabus at key points. That sounds relatively simple, but introducing and sustaining such a programme is not easy. Universities, to begin with, have no tradition of leadership training, nor — until comparatively recently — have their 'sub-cultures' placed any value on it. Secondly, who would teach these transferable personal skills? My work at the University of Surrey, first as Professorial Fellow in Leadership Studies (1979–83) and then as Visiting Professor in the Faculty of Engineering offers some pointers.

In my inaugural lecture at the university in November 1980 (which I was fortunately not invited to deliver until almost two years after my work there had commenced), I put the case as best I could, using the hour-glass model for leadership training along ACL lines, linking it to training in the other key areas of transferable personal skills—communication and general problem-solving, decision making and creative thinking. (Surrey was already giving its engineering students training in communication skills as well as business finance.) Let me quote from my inaugural lecture, where I took the five principles or areas of leadership development which emerged from my work at Sandhurst and discussed each in turn:

The Leadership Course

'There is a need for a short course in leadership studies — one or two days at the most. It should certainly be not less than one day at a time and it should be based on the principles that I have outlined. It should be seen as an essential part of an engineer's or scientist's (or an equivalent discipline's) course, not as something offered in the vacation as an 'optional extra'. Leadership development is a symbiotic activity; it belongs intrinsically with professional preparation.

'The experiments I've done with three engineering departments at the University of Surrey over the last year illustrate the possibilities in this field. The Civil Engineers, the Mechanical Engineers, and the Honours Degree Engineers have each run three programmes in this field based upon the kind of hallmarks which I have described. By way of evaluation, we asked the students several questions at the end of the course, such as, "How would you rate the day in terms of interest and relevance to your job?"

'The below chart suggests that the leadership seminars have a high degree of acceptability from the engineering students. The first programme was a small one composed of just five civil engineers, five mechanical engineers, a chemist and three members of staff. They were recruited by putting a notice on notice-boards asking for volunteers. It was as a result of that pilot first course that the other programmes have developed. The Civil Engineers have already moved to a two-day version and the Mechanical Engineers are thinking much along the same lines.

		As far as interest and relevance to your future working life are concerned, how do you rate this day as a whole?					
		0 poor	20 fair	40 average	60 good	80 very good	100 excellent
VOLUNTEERS (YEAR 4)	(16)	–	–	1	6	9	–
CIVIL ENGINEERS (YEAR 4)	(39)	–	–	1	7	23	8
HONOURS DEGREE ENGINEERS (YEAR 4)	(16)	–	–	3	6	7	–
MECHANICAL ENGINEERS (YEAR 2)	(31)	–	–	–	6	20	5
CIVIL ENGINEERS (YEAR 2)	(28)	–	–	–	10	17	1
HONOURS DEGREE ENGINEERS (YEAR 4)	(11)	–	–	1	5	4	1
TOTALS	141			6	40	80	15

Average: 75

Evaluations of University of Surrey Experimental Courses in Leadership for Engineering Undergraduates.

'We also asked the students to give examples concretely of what they had actually learnt on the day. It is impossible for me to do justice to those replies this evening, but anybody who is professionally interested is most welcome to see them.

'The last question was "Do you recommend this programme to other students at Surrey and elsewhere?" Without exception all 141 students replied that they did so. And then we asked them where they thought these leadership courses ought to come in their syllabus. They divided between those who thought it should come in the final year after the experience in the industrial year, and those who thought it should come before the industrial year so that they could benefit more from that year. Based on their comments and advice we are moving towards the principle of doing it before the industrial year with some sort of "follow-up" session at the beginning of the final year.

Field Leadership Training

'The second heading of my five key areas I called in the military or Sandhurst context field leadership training. There it meant the officer cadet out in the field or exercises with an instructor watching him as he took charge of the platoon and commenting at the end, not simply on the tactics involved but also on the leadership aspect. The bulk of really valuable leadership training took place in the field. How do you apply that principle to a university? Well, I suggest that we should think more of the industrial year as being not simply about technical or professional experience, but also about people. The industrial tutor who visits the students in the course of that year should see himself as being a tutor in the realm of leadership and communication.

Staff Training

'Staff training is essential if tutors are going to be able to give effective comment on leadership during the industrial year. I see it as part of the responsibility of leadership studies in a university to make available some sort of preparation and training for that aspect of the tutor's role.

'Who should actually teach the one or two-day course? My answer is that it should be primarily the professionals concerned, the engineers or the scientists, the members of the particular discipline. Already eight lecturers in the Civil and Mechanical Engineering Departments have embarked on a programme of external leadership courses, preparing them to play a fuller part in developments at the University of Surrey. But we also need to involve managers in our courses. For lecturers are often aware that they lack experience of leadership in management which they can share with people. When we have involved managers from industry on courses, the quality of the learning goes up considerably. Where can we find the managers? Three places suggest themselves: (1) companies and organizations in the neighbourhood of the university; (2) companies which are involved already in terms of taking students in the industrial year; and, (3) from former graduates of the university who are already at work in industry. The Charter of this university speaks of it as being a place where the academic objectives are pursued "in close co-operation with industry". Leadership studies is a marvellous field for that bridge-building between academic and industrial life to take place. Our Charter also speaks about the structure or ethos of the university, and I want to say a word about that in a moment.

Research and Development

'As for research and development, I see a partnership between the academic contribution of leadership studies and the practitioners, the engineers and the managers, to evolve and develop the programme together. At Sandhurst the advisory group took the form of a Leadership Committee. Here in a Faculty or Department, I look for a committed group of lecturers who will work with me to develop this work to relate it more to the actual technical area of study and to see that it ties in with other related aspects of the syllabus — for example, business studies, communication studies and the history of science and technology. Also we need to work together as a staff group to develop our own abilities in leadership development. That is what I mean by "research and development" in this context.

Structure and Ethos

'The structure and ethos of a university is explicable in terms of its purpose, which is the pursuit of learning, just as the structure and ethos of a company is determined by its particular purpose — the production of goods and services for profit. Neither a university nor an industrial company is set up to be a place primarily for the development of leadership. Yet there are aspects in the structure and the ethos of both which can further good leadership. Let me mention some of them.

'Does the structure allow sufficient opportunities for people to work together in groups and perhaps to take charge for a short time? There must be very few undergraduates who haven't been asked in their first selection interview whether or not they have taken part in any undergraduate societies. If so, have they taken a lead in them? As senior staff we cannot do much about student societies, for they are not in our discretion. But we can perhaps extend group project work — activities which involve people working together — where it is possible within the academic syllabus.

'The example of the staff is a very potent force in the atmosphere or the *milieu* in which leadership is learned. The people who take positions of senior responsibility in the university, I believe, should go through some sort of programme of leadership development. This university happens to be something of a pioneer in this field and takes staff development very seriously. Already it has sent two or three future heads of department on external leadership courses. We have also sent some senior technicians on the Action-Centred Leadership courses for scientists, run jointly here and three times a year by the Industrial Society and the University of Surrey. The Chief Technician in the Chemical Engineering Department, for example, attended one last month. I believe passionately in the principle that nobody should be given a job requiring leadership unless they've been given some training or preparation for it.

'There are lecturers who are not in positions of responsibility who still can exercise leadership. Just as the manager of tomorrow needs to incorporate in his make-up something of the university teacher, so also the university lecturer should be something of a leader. Our Charter speaks of this need when it describes the university as a place not merely of "discipline but of inspiration" — a marvellous phrase. Discipline may come through scholarship, but it's the teacher who has something of the leader in him, both in his teaching and in his research, who will generate *inspiration*.

'The Charter speaks also of this university as being a place where people acquire not just knowledge but also wisdom. I should like to reflect on this phrase for a very few moments. Some chemist of the human spirit once analysed this mysterious quality of wisdom into three constituent elements: intelligence, experience and goodness. Intelligence we may take for granted in a university environment. Experience for most of our students is something that largely lies ahead in the future. But what of goodness? Somebody once said that there is a distinction between "good leadership" and "leadership for good". You may feel I have spoken almost entirely of the former, but I believe that a university should be a place where values are explored and discovered. It provides an opportunity for young people to formulate some kind of purpose for their lives.

'In that context I welcome as a complementary development the evolving in the last few years of university industrial societies, of which there are more than 24, including societies in Oxford and Cambridge Universities and at Imperial College in London University. We are hoping to start one in this university. An Industrial Society gives students an opportunity to think about the kind of contribution to society which is made by industry. At best they can convey to the student that there is something immensely worthwhile to be struggled for in the world of work. Thus university industrial societies can be an important ingredient of the ethos of a modern university.

Leaders for Tomorrow

'A few weeks ago a managing director said to me, "I can see that you are preparing students and young managers for today's leadership, but what about tomorrow? Won't the leadership requirement tomorrow be significantly different from that of today?" That is obviously an important question, not just for those of us in this room who are involved in universities and I trust thinking about the development of leadership there. It is also relevant to those of us here who are concerned with the development of young managers who are already at work and yet who are going to be the captains of industry tomorrow. It is not the task of the holder of this Professorial Fellowship in Leadership Studies to answer that question, but I am sure that is one of his responsibilities to stimulate thought about it as widely as possible.

'A university is certainly a good place to explore possible answers. For it is one of the historic functions of a university to review critically and pass on the story or tradition of our culture. Buried within that tradition are insights, examples and ideas about leadership which may be relevant to the future. History is sometimes rather like a musical symphony: a single instrument in a remote part of the orchestra may announce very early a theme which is taken up much later in the score by the whole orchestra.

'Take *humility*, for example, an attribute which is more commonly associated perhaps with great scientists, such as Newton or Einstein, rather than with leaders. But if you look at the tradition — that story of three thousand years of human experience reflected upon by men and women — if you look deeply into that tradition you will find that humility is there in the writings about leadership — "He who would be greatest among you, let him be the servant of all" — "I am among you as one who serves" — "Serve to Lead".

'You may also recall the words of Lao-Tzu, the famous Chinese sage of the sixth century BC who concluded some celebrated verses on this theme by reflecting on the effects which the leader has on the group of followers. His words may carry a meaning for the future, when more people will share in power. If everybody has their little bit of power and we are all equal, what is leadership going to be like? Lao-Tzu ended his verses with these words:

But of a good leader, who talks little,
When his work is done, his aim fulfilled,
They will all say, "We did this ourselves."

'Dag Hammarsksjöld, while he was Secretary-General of the United Nations, kept a journal, later published under the title of *Markings*. One night he wrote an entry in it on the theme of humility and the effect it has on others. He addressed his words to himself but they are relevant to the leader of tomorrow:

"Your position never gives you the right to command. It only imposes on you the duty of so living your life that others may receive your orders without being humiliated."

'In conclusion, I should like to say briefly that I have attempted no more in this inaugural lecture than to persuade you that universities can and should make a significant contribution to the development of tomorrow's leaders.

'Lastly, may I thank you all very much for listening to me with such interest.'

* * *

Seven years have passed since I gave that lecture. During that time, largely through the initiative and leadership of Dr Peter Gardiner in the Department of Civil Engineering, the leadership course has been consolidated and developed within the Faculty of Engineering at the University of Surrey, supported throughout by the Vice-Chancellor, Dr Anthony Kelly FRS. Now more than 1,500 students have been through the course, each completing an evaluation sheet at the end of it. Some twenty lecturers in the Faculty of Engineering are now running that programme from year to year as leadership tutors or trainers, with no direct involvement by me. They have run pilot courses for other universities as well as some courses for engineering firms and for professional bodies, such as the Institute of Chartered Surveyors.

The emergence of this group of leadership tutors is itself an interesting example of team building. Individual academics are able to decide whether or not to devote their marginal time to any particular activity. The task of persuading them of the merits of ACL and then enlisting their support was essential, but the result is an outstanding team of enthusiastic and skilled trainers.

During the third year of the degree course — spent working in industry —students are given an assignment to act as observers of leadership in action and to write a brief case study on what they see or experience in relation to the principles of the functional leadership course. Some of these studies 'on the job' are then selected for discussion on a review day held at the university when the students return to commence their final year. Occasionally students will be given responsibilities which enable them to practise some leadership themselves. Almost all of them have the experience of working in teams where they can learn at first hand about the impact of good — and not-so-good — leadership in management.

In 1987 I was invited to address the Conference of Engineering Professors in British Universities on the subject of leadership development in universities. As a result, a team of leadership trainers from Surrey were given a day on the first national programme designed to equip some twenty lecturers in other university engineering departments to teach the non-technical aspects of becoming an effective engineer. With the support of the Engineering Council and the professional Engineering Institutes there is no reason why a core curriculum for engineering undergraduates in the 'human side of enterprise' should not be developed, along the lines already pioneered in part at the University of Surrey.

CONCLUSION

The change of climate within universities, in respect of attitudes to academic leadership and also the importance of their role in developing leaders, is well summed up in a speech delivered by the Vice-Chancellor of the University of London, Lord Flowers, formerly Principal of Imperial College. The occasion was a residential study group on leadership for the heads of colleges and schools, including the large teaching hospitals, within the university, which I was leading. The address of Lord Flowers included the following extracts:

> 'Early in his book in *Effective Leadership*, John Adair quotes a letter which Field-Marshal Viscount Montgomery wrote to him in 1968.
>
> 'I won't attempt the famous intonation, but I'm sure the rhythm of the sentences will come through: "Leadership is an immense subject. Nowhere is it more important to teach it than at Sandhurst and in our universities; in fact, to youth, since it falls on dead ground with the older generation." I will take that as my text.
>
> 'The more one thinks about Montgomery's assertion, the more extraordinary it becomes. First, of course, there was almost certainly no overt academic teaching of leadership in British universities in 1968. The new universities, together with a few older centres of commercial relevance such as LSE, had barely begun to exert an influence on the system as a whole by their teaching of what might collectively be termed "management studies". Business schools were in their infancy: London's was founded in 1965. So the suggestion of teaching leadership ran quite against the academic tide of the late 1960s.
>
> 'It also ran against the tide of general opinion. Consensus was of course the vogue: nowhere more so than in universities.
>
> 'If an organization's purpose and its future are linked,

then it is not only the present leaders who matter. Indeed, training them in leadership may well be a little beside the point: an old dog may learn an odd new trick, but can rarely change his whole act. We have to look to our leaders of the future. By that, I do not necessarily mean identifying bright individuals in their late twenties who may make it to the top of their institutions — if they stick around for long enough. I mean creating a climate in which leadership can flourish, rather than be restrained by precedent and the safety belt of committee decisions...

'I wish to conclude simply by reminding you of the remark of Montgomery with which I began; that it is most important to teach leadership to youth, since "it falls on dead ground with the older generation." It may be that our most difficult, yet most vital, challenge of leadership is to prepare the next generation to lead.

'May I finish by saying "Thank you" to John Adair for the extremely important work he is doing for universities in general, and for agreeing to lead this particular study group for our university, which contains many fine leaders, some of whom are in this room tonight, but none who could not learn a little more by contact with their fellows.'

KEYPOINTS

- Universities are now foremost among the natural recruiting grounds for tomorrow's leaders in all walks of life.
- A concise programme in transferable personal skills would enhance the education and training of most undergraduates who will work in fields where cooperation is essential. It would counteract the individualism engendered by much academic work.
- All university students should have the opportunity for such a course in leadership, communication skills and creative or innovative thinking. But it should be built into the courses of those disciplines such as engineering and science, that prepare many of the managers of tomorrow.
- Leadership and the other associated skills should be seen as part-and-parcel of becoming a good engineer (or equivalent), not as management training. The programme does form a platform, however, upon which management development can be built later, after some job experience.
- At university the prime aim should be to sow the seeds of leadership and team work. The seeds of the future lie in the present.
- The ten principles of leadership development can be applied within universities.

The test of leadership is not to put greatness into humanity but to elicit it, for the greatness is there already.

John Buchan

5 Transferable Personal Skills

Tact is the ability to make a point without making an enemy.

Increasing importance is being attached in Britain to the skills of graduates in areas outside those of their specialist discipline—what have been called transferable personal skills. I cite below three sources:

1. The University Grants Committee's document, 'A strategy for Higher Education into the 1990s' (September 1984).

   This began with a chapter entitled 'Higher Education and the Needs of Society', and was written with the National Advisory Board which is responsible for Polytechnics. It includes these words:

   > 'Specific knowledge quickly becomes outdated and the context in which it is applied rapidly changes. Initial higher education, particularly at diploma and first degree level, should therefore emphasize underlying intellectual, scientific and technological principles rather than provide too narrow a specialist knowledge. The abilities most valued in industrial, commercial and professional life as well as in public and social administration are the transferable intellectual and personal skills. These include the ability to analyse complex issues, to identify the core of a problem and the means of solving it, to synthesize and integrate disparate elements, to clarify values, to make effective use of numerical and other information, to work cooperatively and constructively with others and, above all perhaps, to communicate clearly both orally and in writing. A higher education system which provides its students with these skills is serving society well.'

2. The Royal Society of Arts has for some time been active in promoting its 'Education for Capability' theme. Its aim is to encourage and develop in people four capacities that are currently under-emphasized in our education system. It lists four attributes thus:

'The great majority of learners—whether pupils at school, students at universities, polytechnics or college, or adults still wanting to learn—are destined for a productive life of practical action. They are going to do things, design things, make things, organize things, for the most part in cooperation with other people. They need to improve their *Competence*, by the practice of skills and the use of knowledge; to *Cope* better with their own lives and the problems that confront them and society; to develop their *Creative* abilities; and, above all, to *Cooperate* with other people.'

3. The Conference of British Industry, in its evidence to the Parlimentary Committee on Education in 1980, said:

   'The complaint which we frequently get from companies is that ... the people who come out of technological disciplines are all too often less lively as people than those who have done less relevant subjects like the arts... We would like to see somewhat greater weight attached to the personal qualities, such as motivation, ability for original thought and ability to get at and solve problems.'

I believe these views form a useful background to my proposals to universities.

* * *

There is a strong evidence that the better employers of graduates look for a good degree in engineering and signs of transferable personal skills. These skills, abilities or qualities fall, I suggest, into five broad categories:

- leadership and teamwork.
- communication skills (speaking, listening, writing, and reading).
- decision-making; thinking skills in the applied forms of problem-solving, decision-making, and innovative thinking.
- self-management; the ability to organize oneself; time-management skills; learning skills.
- personal qualities; desirable qualities of personality and character, such as energy, enthusiasm and initiative.

All universities would claim that they teach their students the transferable skill of thinking analytically and critically about issues and problems. But the opportunities for developing some of the other skills mentioned are more variable. As explained in the last chapter, the University of Surrey has probably done more in these other areas than most universities.

THE ENGINEERING CONTEXT

It looks as if the Institutions and the Engineering Council will increasingly require all university engineering disciplines to include a programme in the non-technical aspects of becoming a graduate engineer. I believe that we should be developing a core curriculum in this area. Only the core would be the same for all: individual universities and departments would be free to adapt the core curriculum to suit their requirements within some broad limits. I suggest:

- The programme should be kept short in length (not more than 200 hours), but should be excellent as far as content and training methods are concerned.
- The content should focus upon the 'big three' personal transferable skills — leadership and teamwork, communication, and creative problem-solving — which have been identified as essential or desirable in an engineer. The fact that they are also the seeds of management should be regarded as a bonus.
- The approach should be practical and participative. Courses should not be 'academic'.
- It follows from the above principles that these courses should be taught by lecturers in engineering (supported by engineers and managers from industry), not by service teaching from other academic disciplines, such as management studies.
- In order to be effective as teachers in this non-technical field, lecturers in engineering departments will need leadership training and support. Hence the need for a director of studies in each university in this area who will act as a focus for the research and advisory function.

THE EMPLOYERS' VIEWS

In 1985 the Standing Conference of Employers of Graduates (SCOEG) published a survey on 'What employers look for in their graduate recruits.' The questionnaire was completed by 84 organizations, representing an annual recruitment of 6,150 graduates. Members were invited to cite initiatives taken in higher education which they thought particularly helpful. Particular mention was made of the leadership courses at Surrey University.

Personal transferable, skills are thought to be of high importance in most employments to which graduates are recruited, the report concluded. Skills of communication, both oral and in writing, are those most lacking in graduate recruits. Higher education institutions could do more to encourage the development of these skills, though some respondents doubted the will or the wish of academics to achieve major changes.

My own research did not extend to the transferable personal skills that employers look for when recruiting from schools or the various youth training schemes. But *Transition*, the journal of the British Association of Commercial and Industrial Education (BACIE), published in June 1987 this account of some relevant research:

In 1986 I was commissioned to carry out a further survey of transferable personal skills by a DES-funded project called Pegasus, set up to provide optional courses for undergraduates in this area. (As part of the Pegasus research programme I designed and led two pilot schemes for Churchill College, Cambridge, and for the University of York, which included leadership training weekends at Brathay Hall and in the Yorkshire Dales.) I looked at the lists of qualities/abilities identified by: BOC, STC, British Rail, an IBM colloquium of industrialists on 'Preparing Tomorrow's Leaders', a London Borough, the Civil Service Selection Board, May & Baker, Shell, SCOEG, and some assessment centres. I grouped them under five headings:

1. *Leadership and Teamwork*
   Teamwork/team membership; planning and organizing; cooperation; consistent and dependable behaviour; wins gracefully; expresses hostility tactfully; delegates frequently/effectively; initiates; controls and coordinates; gets on with others.
2. *Communication Skills*
   Speaking; perceptive listening; written communication; persuasiveness; arguing assertively, not aggressively.
3. *Decision-Making*
   Creativity; power of analysis; critical judgement; reasoning; inquiring mind; speed of uptake; analytic reasoning skills; imagination; sense of reality; helicopter view.
4. *Self-Management*
   Self-motivation/initiative; sets and achieves goals; works under pressure; works to deadline; self-awareness; achievement-motivated.
5. *Personal Qualities*
   Strong but not dominating personality; tenacity and determination; personal impact and presentation; good appearance; resilience under pressure; maturity for age; flexibility and adaptability; vigour and energy; reliable, stable, calm, cool; breadth of interest.

This list of abilities and qualities can be adapted (see Appendix C) for training purposes in order to encourage discussion — and some self-assessment. With those aims in mind — I have used them in the context of the above-mentioned leadership training courses for undergraduates from Cambridge and York Universities.

> *One other thing stirs me when I look back at my youthful days, the fact that so many people gave me something or were something to me without knowing it.*
>
> *Albert Schweitzer*

WHAT EMPLOYERS LOOK FOR IN SCHOOL LEAVERS

The Polytechnic of Wales conducted a survey of all the companies in the area employing over 200 people. Employers were asked to rate the importance of 20 personal and educational factors when considering a school leaver for employment. The table below shows the percentages for each factor, in order of importance. It gives a good indication of the kinds of young people industry is looking for.

	Very or quite important %	Important %	Not very important %
Reliability and trustworthiness	91	7	2
Punctuality	91	9	0
Willingness to learn	88	9	3
Ability to work as a member of a team	85	14	1
Enthusiasm	82	17	1
Clean and tidy appearance	78	20	2
Ability to work with minimum supervision	61	33	1
Initiative	59	34	7
Ability to work with figures	56	30	14
Ability to write clearly and concisely	52	38	10
Well organized	52	42	6
Ability to speak fluently/with confidence	51	40	9
Friendliness	44	44	12
Some qualifications related to job	35	22	43
Good 'O' level/CSE in academic subjects	30	31	39
Qualifications in vocational subjects	23	36	41
Good dress sense	23	38	39
Some general work experience	23	22	55
Creativity	22	46	34
Work experience related to job	21	16	63

KEYPOINTS

- Transferable personal skills — the skills employers look for in graduates and school leavers — can be broken down into five clusters:
  - leadership and teamwork
  - communication skills
  - decision-making
  - self-management
  - personal qualities.
- It is possible to offer students at university, college or school opportunities for developing these abilities, and it is desirable to do so, especially for those intending to enter industry and commerce.
- In order to become effective providers of this form of training, universities must first recognize its value and then make provision for a director in each university (In 1987 the University of Surrey made the first appointment of this kind.)
- Close partnership with industry and commerce in this area of development training pays dividends to both universities and employers.
- Britain should have introduced the changes advocated here some twenty years ago. Why did it not happen?
- The leaders of tomorrow — the twenty-first century — are in homes, schools, colleges and universities today. They will need to be good leaders as well as leaders for good.

> *The person who can combine intelligence and humanity with a genuine enthusiasm is likely to be a true leader.*
>
> *Roger Falk*

6 The Head Teacher as Leader

We are they who help to make or mar all. They that are the flower of our nation, and those who become leaders of all the rest, are committed to our education and instruction.

John Brinsley, writing to his fellow schoolmasters in 'A Consolation for Our Grammar Schools,' 1622

One of the most important extensions of ACL in recent years has been its application to training head teachers, where it has proved to be extremely useful.

This development began in 1970. As head of the Leadership Department at the Industrial Society that year I organized a day-long seminar on the subject, which more than 100 head teachers from both public and private sectors attended.

THE 'HEAD AS LEADER' CONFERENCE

After a short introduction and welcome the conference broke up into 15 small groups for discussion. The first question I put to them was 'What are the essential leadership qualities of a head teacher?' It produced a long list of attributes, ranging from vision, compassion and humility to 'low cunning' and 'the desirability of being young, defiant, mobile, and cosmopolitan'! The second question — 'What are the true aims and purposes of education?' — also produced a thought-provoking crop of replies from the small discussion groups.

After two presentations by me on leadership and communication, the conference again divided into fifteen small groups to digest the three circles and the functional leadership approach, including motivation, decision-making, and communication in organizations. They reported back on the actions they intended to take and any problems or questions they wished to raise.

Points arising from the afternoon group discussion included:

Install a consultative committee.

Reconsider the role of the deputy head.

Look at the prefect system again.

Are briefing groups practicable in a staff of 30, or will they be divisive?

Sift and investigate communications.

Job definition for heads of departments.

Who decides what is intrinsically worthwhile?

Written objectives for staff.

When should the head not be a leader?

Define the chain of authority.

Identify 'leader' for each member of staff (and recognize that 'father/mother' figures emerge).

Study staff motivation.

Size of staff meetings?

What is the head's role in linking school and community education?

Democratization — to what extent is it possible? To what extent is it desirable?

Should school reflect society or mould it?

Level of personal relationship of head with staff — should head enter staffroom without knocking?

Clarify aims and objectives.

More consultation with staff — involvement in ideas.

More positive line on decision-making.

A more broadly based experience for teachers.

Make time for briefing meetings.

To whom is the head accountable? Who is the head's boss?

More monitoring/caring.

In school there is an equal professional standing among staff. Is this not different from vertical management structure If so it affects the chain of command.

Problem of apathy with proliferation of committees and councils.

Creating small working groups.

Definition of objectives and accountability.

The day had clearly been significant for a number of those present. For example, among the letters I received afterwards from participants detailing their action plans came one from the head of a large comprehensive secondary school in an inner city area:

- I shall with greater confidence be decisive in my role as a leader e.g. the lead required between the 'young turk' on the one hand and the older colleague on the other.
- I am confirmed in the idea to set up a communication system, based on the idea of downward briefing groups and upward consultative meetings.
- I shall ask specifically for each head of department's aims and objectives of his or her department.
- I shall ask regularly for the heads of department minutes of meetings and take up the option to be invited sometimes.

THE REPORT *TEN GOOD SCHOOLS* (1977)

The Industrial Society did not follow up the 1970 seminar. That was partly due to my absence, as I left the Society that year in order to do some more research and writing at Oxford. Another reason, I suspect, was a sense of complacency in and about the educational system which meant that training for head teachers—or any teachers—was at that time extremely low on the national agenda.

A report that should have changed that climate and put leadership back on the map was published in 1977 by H.M. Inspectorate of Schools, entitled *Ten Good Schools*. Having made a list of 50 schools known to be 'good', the Inspectorate selected ten for diversity and tried to figure out what they had in common. The answer was simple: good schools have good heads. The report characterized them as follows:

'These schools see themselves as places designed for learning; they take trouble to make their philosophies *explicit* for themselves and to *explain* them to parents and pupils; the foundation of their work and corporate life is an acceptance of shared values.

'Emphasis is laid on *consultation*, team work and participation, but without exception, the most important single factor in the success of these schools is the quality of *leadership* at the head. Without exception, the heads have qualities of *imagination* and *vision*, tempered by realism, which have enabled them to sum up not only their present situation but also attainable future goals. They appreciate the need for specific educational aims, both social and intellectual, and have the capacity to communicate these to staff, pupils and parents, to win their assent and to put their own *policies* into practice. Their sympathetic understanding of staff and pupils, their acceptability, good *humour* and sense of *proportion* and their *dedication to their task* has won them the respect of parents, teachers and taught. Conscious of the corruption of power and though ready to take final responsibility, they have made power-sharing the keynote of their organization and administration. Such leadership is crucial for success and these schools are what their heads and staffs have made them.'

The implication of *Ten Good Schools* was simple. The secondary educational system in this country – like the Services, industry or commerce – needed to grow leaders. But developing leaders, as we have seen in Part One, is more than a matter of organizing courses. It requires a strategy. In fact weight must be given to each of the ten principles or steps within the system. Take the principle of *selection* as an example.

SELECTING THE HEAD TEACHER

A further report, the culmination of three years research funded by the government, highlighted the importance of leadership *selection* in this field. Its title, *The Most Important Thing We Do*, is the description chief education officers most commonly gave the researchers of their part in choosing school heads.

They and the local politicians and school governors who also took part in the selection processes accepted that the quality of the head teacher is the main factor in a school's success or failure. They also knew, many said, that when they appoint a head at the age of about 40 to run a school which, on average, then cost just under £1 million a year to run, they were making the single most important decision affecting an investment of some £18 million.

He or she will be almost impossible to move for 20 years. On average, chief education officers said that about 10 per cent of heads appointed were 'duds'. In one unnamed authority the chief education officer concerned reckoned that was true of a quarter of all local headship appointments!

The researchers found no procedures common to all authorities; no chief education officers trained in modern techniques for filling senior jobs. Preliminary interviews with chief education officers 'rarely' followed good interview practice and were generally not properly recorded.

All in all, concluded the researchers, 'the dominant characteristic of local education authority procedures is that they are conducted almost exclusively in the dark.'

A 10 per cent rate of 'duds' is far too high. If leadership selection is done properly it should be no more than 2 or 3 per cent. And, of course, there should be some means of removing heads who do not come up to the minimum standards of competence as managers.

That was more than ten years ago and perhaps things have changed dramatically for the better since then. Certainly selecting heads needs to be done by subjecting them to some latter-day version of the War Office Selection Board Interview method. Justice has to be not only done but seen to be done.

In 1985 Harry Tomlinson, Principal of Margaret Ashton College in Manchester, wrote to me to say that 'I have suggested to the Secretary of State for Education and Science that the establishment of a National Secondary Headship Assessment Centre would provide a useful addition to other proposals for improving the selection of secondary heads, a matter he clearly feels very strongly about.' I agreed with him.

ACL FOR HEADS AND COLLEGES: A CASE STUDY

In 1982 the Industrial Society initiated a series of courses entitled Leadership in Schools and Colleges.

The Society invited me to speak at one of their conferences in 1985 for Local Education Authorities about this programme.

During the day I heard the following talk given by Fred Pape, Headmaster of Queen Elizabeth's High School in Gainsborough. It forms a not untypical case study of the effect of leadership training on a head teacher's approach to running a school:

'I run one of the remaining 147 grammar schools in England. It was formed only in 1983 by the amalgamation of two single-sex grammar schools to become the largest grammar school in Lincolnshire with a roll of 800, including over 150 in the Sixth Form. I had previously been head of the Boys' Grammar School since 1977, and before that head of Lower School in a Cambridgeshire comprehensive, Rector of the Anglo-Colombian School at Bogota, Colombia, and first Deputy Head of a Nottinghamshire comprehensive.

'I had been on management courses, but my style and ideas of management were based almost entirely on experience, particularly on my experience in Colombia where there were no chief inspectors, chief advisers, or senior advisers, and where I and my team of English and Colombian teachers controlled all aspects of one of the best-equipped and most prestigious schools on the South American continent, a region where hair-raising financial instability and the doctrine of mañana are the rule. From Bogota, I learnt independence, I learnt the importance of sound financial management, and I thought I had learnt much about how to manage teaching and ancillary staff.

'In April 1983, I was selected for the ACL course. I should have liked to have to known the basis on which I and eleven other Lincolnshire heads were selected. I have always comforted myself that it was because I was about to take on a much larger school and needed the training, rather than that I was among twelve heads who were such disasters that our re-training was top priority!

'I found the two-day course and its one-day follow-up painful, refreshing and inspiring. Painful because it made me realize how haphazard and illogical my previous management style had been; refreshing because it made me re-examine every aspect of my headship; and inspiring because I realized that it was a total philosophy — not something from which one could take ideas in isolation. It has given me a strategy for working instead of my previous hotch-potch of good and bad practice.

* * *

'ACL practice dictates that I now indicate that the meat of my short dissertation is to deal with particular aspects of my work in which ACL has changed my attitudes and practices radically. The time of the afternoon dictates that I make these aspects as graphic, colourful, and brief as possible!

'First, *thinking time*. I still tend to fill all my time, partly because I am a product of a family background which believed that idleness was synonymous with laziness, but I do deliberately leave my study to walk round the campus, listen to pupils and try to see different aspects of problems. Incidentally, following the ACL practices on delegation seems to have meant that I now get only the difficult problems. I would dearly love to take a lunch break, but that remains a distant prospect in these turbulent times. For thinking time, moments of peace at home have to suffice, but I have come to recognize that thinking time must be found so that I can detach myself for a while and try to take a more distant view of my school. Only then do the really important things emerge and the unimportant ones fade into the background. All headteachers need vision: I do not think it attainable without regular thinking time.

'Secondly, *delegation*. I have always found delegation and the involvement of all staff in the task rather elusive—not because I feel threatened, nor because I doubt the abilities of those around me, but because of the difficulty of monitoring and possibly having to pick up the pieces afterwards. Yet the values and importance of delegating are not lost upon me. I have instituted all the machinery for delegation: (1) an Academic Board meeting monthly and advising on all curriculum aspects, (2) an Operational Research Unit of six (myself, two Deputies and three Heads of Year), meeting weekly and examining all aspects of the running of the school, and (3) a daily meeting with my Deputies to prepare for the assemblies and the day ahead.

'Departments meet at least once a term: year tutors meet fortnightly; and a weekly bulletin keeps everyone informed of all aspects of school life, yet the one completely democratic forum I keep to a minimum: the Staff Meeting. I found Staff Meetings mentally exhausting and looked upon them as a necessary exercise which rarely simplified or brought inspiration to the school's general aims. We meet as a staff of fifty once a term—more often if necessary — and I now follow ACL advice with care:

- I prepare the agenda well in advance and publicize it, having invited contributions from all.
- I make clear that what I say initially is policy and that what conclusions the meeting may come to later are advisory. I do this because a discussion involving fifty rarely comes to a conclusion of any kind.
- I arrange seating in a very large circle.
- I provide free tea and buns.
- I take Any Other Business items as being items for the agenda of the next meeting.
- I start on time and specify a finishing time.
- I chair the meeting and insist on apologies in person to myself.
- And after my initial input, I leave my deputies to put the hierarchy line, concentrating on directing the discussion, trying to summarize, and trying to select good points to applaud and adopt.

'The ACL course brought to me a priceless gift: a means of measuring partial success in influencing and motivating staff. When a breach occurred in relationships, I used to feel that I had failed. Now I can see that breach as a faltering and know that it is part of the continuous process of building the team and of developing the individual. A previously nebulous concept of management has taken on form and structure. I now believe that all members of staff can be influenced and led albeit slowly and probably unwillingly along a road towards a definable goal.

'At this time, I lean heavily on this aspect of ACL. My school is at present the only grammar school in England actively involved in a Training and Vocational Education Initiative Scheme. The task is to produce a TVEI package which the Manpower Services Commission would fund with £1.8 million. In this exercise, the ACL guidelines will play a crucial part.

'I believe that the ACL training enables a headteacher to fulfil his leadership role with more purpose, more understanding and in a much more structured fashion. It has given me a workable, progressive method of improving my school and I can see that it will continue to stand me in good stead in coping with the TVEI initiative, and with other initiatives still to come.'

* * *

In a letter to me Mr Pape added these interesting comments:

> 'I wonder if you have developed further your philosophy of management: it seems to me that since we met in London, there has been such an extension of the school manager's responsibilities that your philosophy becomes *more* important, but also more difficult to put into practice. The scope of a headteacher's duties grows more wide-ranging and the follow-up to the delegation — which is ever more required — more difficult.
>
> 'I was thinking some time ago of the changing nature of educational management: how the widening of its sphere of control is forcing headteachers out of their purely educational role and also leading to a diversification of interests. The manager's ability in particular to develop individuals is being reduced by his preoccupation with the extension of his role. This can only be detrimental to staff morale and involvement. Your ACL guidelines say: 'Train and develop people, particularly the young,' but the opportunities to do so are more and more limited by static staffing. I wonder how you see us solving this problem: if the opportunities to develop the young and give them a larger say in the running of the school are fewer, how can we train and develop them? I have formed a time-tabling committee to involve them in understanding the implementation of the curriculum, but what they must have is practical involvement in day-to-day organization.'

PROGRESS REPORT

It was fortunate that among the delegates on that first course in March 1982 led by Richard Boult, were Dr Michael Rymer, Deputy Head of St Albans School, and Richard Morgan, Headmaster of Cheltenham College. 'They were the first of many educationalists who have guided us,' writes Richard Boult, 'showing how school management—and especially schools' perceptions of management — differ from that in, say, industry. For example David Pert, Headmaster of Brislington School, Bristol coined the phrase the 'organ transplant reject syndrome', stressing that getting the terminology right is important to teachers if the ideas are to be accepted and that syndrome is to be avoided.

> 'A head being sold on the novel idea of appraisal interviews anticipated considerable resistance from his slightly old fashioned common room. He announced that as a busy man he could offer "work review and career development interviews" to the most senior members of staff. Within one term he had to be persuaded to offer the same privilege to all members of staff.'

More than 700 heads have now attended ACL courses organized by the Industrial Society, many of them run on an in-house basis. Local Education Authorities have usually arranged courses on their premises, while private schools often join up with neighbouring schools. Some even invite managers from local industry to participate.

Despite 'the organ transplant reject syndrome' head teachers today are having a great deal of management theory and systematic management development thrust down their throats. Much of this jargon is inappropriate to the world of schools. This is one area where people are all-important. Of course the head teacher must learn to manage resources — money and plant — but the emphasis should be put upon leadership and leadership training. For good leadership is the key to excellence in primary and secondary schools.

> *Example is the school of mankind, and they will learn at no other.*
>
> *Edmund Burke*

KEYPOINTS

- The head teacher occupies a leadership role. He or she should be selected and trained with that chief responsibility in mind.
- Apart from exemplifying the qualities of a good teacher a head should possess a sense of direction, enthusiasm, integrity, warmth and be firm but fair. A certain toughness over standards wins respect.
- Central to the head's role is the ability to help the whole school to achieve its common purpose, maintain and build it as a community, and to meet the individual needs of the least of its members.
- A head's leadership extends to everyone who works in the school community, but a priority is to encourage the staff to see themselves as the school's leadership team.
- Self-development is the main method by which a head becomes a more effective leader and manager: it is learning on the job and through the job. Courses are ancillary.
- Management development needs to be replaced by leadership development as the principal concept in the teaching profession. For the management model of industry and commerce is inappropriate to education, except in marginal ways.

> *There is small risk a leader will be regarded with contempt by those he leads if, whatever he may have to preach, he shows himself best able to perform.*
>
> *Xenophon*

7 Leadership Training in Schools

Experience is the best of schoolmasters, only the school fees are heavy.

Thomas Carlyle

Can leadership be taught in schools? If so, should it be taught?

Perhaps I should say at the outset of this chapter that I have always been rather sceptical about the value of leadership training in schools. By 'leadership training' in this context I mean a planned, formal attempt to teach leadership by means of a kind of course that I was advocating in universities a few pages ago.

The reason for my scepticism stems from the part that *experience* plays in training. Principles or ideas (theory) need experience (practice) for clothing: it is the interplay between the two that produces learning. What may seem a simple, even trite point takes on new meaning in the light of experience. Without that element of experience and the wider, deeper knowledge we call maturity I have always suspected that the leadership exercises on the ACL course would be perceived as mere games by school children. There are times to learn things in life, and I have taken the view that around 18 or 19 years is the right age to learn about leadership in a conceptual way. Pushing life's natural learning times backwards artificially, producing old heads on young shoulders, seems to me a questionable activity. It would be a pity if students arrived at university and said 'But we have done leadership at school!' They may have 'done' it, but it would probably have been at a superficial level, due to lack of experience more than anything else.

THE PRIMARY ROLE OF SCHOOLS IN LEADERSHIP DEVELOPMENT

This scepticism on my part does not mean that I think schools have no contribution to make. On the contrary, I see their role in fostering leadership and team work, communicating and the mental abilities needed for decision-making, problem-solving and creative thinking, as of immense importance. When it comes to schools I would start first with three of the ten steps or principles of leadership development outlined in Part One and leave training courses for students last on the list.

The first of those three steps — the chief executive — I have already discussed in the last chapter. The head teacher, who is in effect the school's chief executive, should be a good leader. A by-product of being a good leader and a leader for good is that the head will be teaching leadership by example. Leadership is caught as much as it is taught.

Secondly, the 'organizational climate' or culture of the school should be such that leadership — as opposed to domineering, bullying, bossing about—is valued and encouraged by all the staff.

Thirdly, the school should be so structured that there are plenty of opportunities to lead. That embraces school appointments, such as form captains and prefects, games captains, chairing or leading school societies — especially debating societies — and project activities like organizing a play or a party.

Within the context of such a school it can make sense to give students the opportunity of participating in a course or conference on leadership and teamwork.

MALVERN SCHOOL: A CASE STUDY

In 1978 the then headmaster of Malvern School, Martin Rogers, asked me to carry out a study of his school to see if leadership training could be introduced. I spent about ten days in all at the school, interviewing staff and students and getting to know the place. As a result of my report a number of changes were introduced. The following year I was invited by Martin Rogers to talk on the subject of leadership development to the conference of headmasters of all the independent schools. The extracts below are from a letter I wrote to Malvern after my initial visits, giving him a sketchmap of my main impressions:

Introduction

'Leadership training as practised by, say, the Industrial Society, is inappropriate because of the lack of experience and no immediate follow-up practice in a leadership appointment.

'Therefore we are thinking more of laying broad foundations — education for leadership rather than skills training in the narrow sense. That embraces: taking responsibility, working with others to achieve a task (as leader, colleague or subordinate) — communicating effectively (both speaking and listening)—decision-making and problem-solving, with creative thinking. This is not an exhaustive list, but it covers the key areas of "the human side of enterprise".

'There is a vague but real sense that you are in the business of developing leadership in this broader sense as well as academic/sports potential. The written comments by the nine boys in my discussion group revealed (in their answers to the questions "What is and what ought to be the purpose of Malvern?") that they were all aware of this area of purpose alongside the examinations hurdle race, which I found interesting. They also, however, shared the awareness of yourself and the staff members that there was a deficiency in this major field. This sense was fed by another vague but real feeling that the world outside, especially industry, was changing and what was needed included a realistic picture of it and a preparation for it, which was seen to include leadership at least for a large number of pupils at the school.

Purpose and Structure

'The structure, or way in which an organism or organization is articulated and works, usually reflects an understanding of the purpose, or at least some unconscious or semi-conscious assumptions about it. By "purpose" I mean the answer to the question "What is this body for?" It is a general statement, and can usually be broken down into more specific aims (or areas of purpose), like light refracted into a spectrum of colours.

'Both my fellow consultant and I put down "a clearer understanding of purpose" at the top of our lists quite independently, for from that would flow — for example — a greater willingness to look thoroughly at how the school actually works to help/hinder leadership development.

'One tangible point that occurs to me is that some sort of card will be needed on which a record of a boy's opportunities of taking responsibility is kept. So that there would be a structural method of recording (and helping to integrate) a boy's passage through the variety of chances to lead that will be increasingly there in his five years at the school.

Leadership Course

'Our discussions over curriculum raised a question in my mind. Will the bulk of masters and boys take leadership seriously if it is not focussed in some way in one or two sessions during the 9-5 curriculum? I do not envisage anything like the various industrial leadership courses, still less potted social studies. Possibly a discussion along the lines of the one I led, followed by a film or case study or practical exercise, all related to the experience which you very rightly said is present in abundant measure in a school like Malvern. Certainly not more than one day, single or split into two halves. This would require experiments. Perhaps I should add that I do not see this area as a priority, and if it causes any anxieties would be happy to put it at the bottom of the list.

Practical Training in Leadership

'About 90 per cent of education for leadership lies here. It means, of course, that boys have practical opportunities (distilled into experience) to take charge or work together in teams. I make a distinction between (a) such times where there is some discussion appraisal or feedback on how it went (from boys and/or masters) and (b) "free-range" times where there is no observer or organized discussion. The realities are such that (b) is likely to predominate, and that is probably no bad thing. There are five key areas of opportunity:

(a) House
 There are different ways of increasing both the quantity and quality of leadership education in the houses. The houses are a central feature of Malvern, and a major part of leadership development is already happening in them all, so this is a question of building on strengths.

(b) Sports and Societies
There is a clear mandate in the school for handing over more responsibility to boys, but the "whys and hows" need to be worked out with the masters and boys involved.

(c) Academic
Not a high priority, but might include such possibilities as classroom administration, group projects, visits, and library responsibilities.

(d) The Combined Cadet Force
The possibilities here are widely recognized, and there are good developments already happening.

(e) School based
Especially school prefects.

Staff Training

'Without giving the staff the opportunity to learn more about leadership development nothing substantial and lasting will be achieved. I was very impressed by the thoughtful observations made to me by members of the staff: obviously the process of opening minds to new ideas and methods has already begun. Some, however, have doubts as to how far they themselves, as "old dogs", can learn "new tricks". This task must be attempted.

'Besides addressing themselves to specific jobs, the Leadership Working Party should also be looking all the time at the wood, not the trees—the whole evolutionary broad front moves forwards, not the individual meetings, events or areas. The LWP can more fruitfully fulfil this role, and carry on the good work when the external consultants are no longer involved, if they are going into the subject more deeply. That means seminars, reading and visits.

Conclusion

'In this area solutions cannot be imposed, and my colleague and I should concentrate on working with groups to identify the problems and shared ways forward. Some may find this participative approach a little disturbing, however mild it would be. One of your oversights might be to watch this particular aspect very carefully, so that we do not misjudge the ethos of the school in this respect. We should, indeed, have to be guided by you (as author and "owner" of the project) on the whole strategy but especially to ensure that we do not overlook or leave behind people in the school community. It is a slow old business, this change, and I do not foresee any problems of going too fast! However, it is people's perceptions that matter, and good communication about what we are up to is a vital dimension of the success of the project.'

* * *

As a result of my final report Malvern experimented with a short leadership course in November 1979. Simon Wilkinson, the Careers Master, sent me this report:

> 'It was as well that I waited until after our report-back session on Monday, December 3rd, before sending you a full report. My colleagues in many cases found that their impressions of what the boys had thought and of what their suggestions would be for improvements were actually contradicted at the follow-up sessions which they held with them. I enclose the programme which we followed for our day-and-a-half. Most seemed to feel that a day-and-a-half at about half term in the first term of the first year sixth is the right time for such a course. Boys have settled down but have not yet become too immersed in their work or got to know each other too well for the effect to be reduced. On the administration side we have got to take more care to see that there is less disruption of classes next year than on the first occasion. We will probably combine this day-and-a-half with our Challenge of Industry conference for the second year sixth next year.
>
> 'The programme itself started with some introductory remarks from George Chesterton, the second master, in the

absence of Martin Rogers who had to attend a memorial service in London. After those remarks I set the scene and we adjourned into our small groups to tackle the question "What is leadership?" and "What makes an effective leader/follower?" These small groups then reported back to larger groups, each composed of three of the small groups. Following this report-back one of the tutors was responsible for the lecture and discussion on the qualities, situational and functional approaches, and for introducing the three circles approaches to leadership. After break there came the first rather unsuccessful exercise "The Photograph". Instead of taking the half-hour suggested, some groups completed it in about five minutes. The ingenuity of the tutors was thereupon tested! Most of them came up with very good additional ideas for filling the time after they had explained the role of leaders and, in particular, of observers. With my group I used the "Indivisible Load" exercise. [These and similar exercises are to be found in the *Handbook of Management Exercises*, published by the British Association of Commercial and Industrial Education (BACIE) in London.]

'After lunch the groups did two outdoor exercises which were of the poles and planks variety, and had been adapted from some which the RAF had suggested. Although initially testing, most groups found that the time allowed was too great, and that the exercises were usually completed early. The appraisal sessions after these and other exercises were very worthwhile, and most tutors thought that boys took part sensibly.

'The next morning we started with the planks and barrels exercise from Action-Centred Leadership which was undoubtedly the most successful of the exercises since it put the participants under most stress because no one completed it in time. This was followed by "Camfam" which again seems to have been a success. Following summing-up sessions in the large groups after break, David Gilbert-Smith from the Leadership Trust brought it all to a conclusion with a brief and good talk.

'Most of the boys seemed to have enjoyed themselves and to have seen the relevance of what they were doing to what is likely to happen after Malvern. It seems that much still needs to be done to ensure that similar experiences and lessons are encountered at Malvern, and that the type of appraisal which we used during the one-and-a-half days is also used by our colleagues in charge of a variety of activities.'

UPPER SIXTH FORM CONFERENCE ON LEADERSHIP (REPTON SCHOOL)

In 1981 Gerry Pellow, the Head of the Careers Department at Repton came to see me at the University of Surrey in order to get my advice and help in running a leadership conference for the sixth form. The conference took place in January 1982 and Gerry Pellow sent me this account of it:

'Repton's eight sixth form conference was held in January 1982 and took as its theme "Leadership". Its aim was to introduce boys and girls in their final year at school to "action-centred leadership" in order to give them some understanding of how tasks are achieved, teams are built and maintained and individual qualities are used and personal satisfactions gained in fulfilling a task.

'The Chairman of the conference was Sandy Ellvers-Dix, formerly of the Industrial Society and a former colleague of Professor John Adair, who holds the Chair of Leadership Studies at the University of Surrey. She chaired the conference, in the words of one of the sixth form delegates, in a "composed, lively, knowledgeable and encouraging way, with excellent organization and a fine sense of humour; all of which demonstrated, admirably, true leadership."

'As in previous years, the conference style revolved around brief lectures, practical case studies and, most important, syndicate discussions. The lectures this year covered such topics as "Leadership in the '80s", "Approaches to Leadership" and "Analysis of Leadership Style". The case studies involved "Jig-Saw", "Mast Contract", "Riskit" (involving creative enterprise) and fourthly "Lost at Sea", all presented, as has become a feature of recent conferences, by the Derby and Derbyshire Junior Chamber of Commerce.

'Reactions from the sixth formers to the case studies were very mixed, partly varying according to the cases themselves, and partly, more significantly, to the degree with which the students were able to carry out one of the techniques of action-centred leadership, namely "observation of the task being carried out and of the way in which a leader worked; how a group was controlled and how individuals in the group contributed." The delegates were much more at home when participating themselves in the tasks. Nevertheless, the comments from a random sample of the boys and girls in response to questioning about what they learned about themselves are significant. They included:

"I found it difficult to learn about my own qualities."
"I do not say enough."
"I had ideas but not enough conviction."
"I learned about balance of qualities."
"I found I was better organized than I thought."
"I now believe in myself."
"I must be more positive."
"I am now less reluctant to take things on."
"I realized some of my weaknesses that I'll keep to myself, thank you."

'Throughout the exercises and discussions, most sixth formers, it seems, became more acutely aware than hitherto of the need to plan, organize and specify tasks, to use all members of a team, to delegate responsibility, and especially how to react with and to others:

"Teamwork was more important than I thought."
"A small amount of encouragement can go a surprisingly long way."
"I needed coordination and subtlety."
"I had to beware of the destroyer."
"We all in our group felt we had to be involved."

'The last comment above, in a way, is a tribute to the other major feature of the conference, viz. the participation of sixteen visiting group advisers who this year included two Old Reptonians and representatives from such diverse organizations as United Biscuits, three breweries, the Derbyshire Constabulary and Marks and Spencer in addition to a lecturer in movement studies and an M.Sc. course psychologist from the University of Hull. The role of these advisers was to spend a day and a half with their teams of sixth formers, individually drawn from the houses and the academic disciplines to form heterogeneous groups; and to cajole, interest and help them preferably as much from the back seat as possible. They play a vital part in the effectiveness of the conference and all the sixth formers who took part in the sample questionnaire were unanimous in their praise of the insights and help given by a splendid team this year:

"He put us at our ease."
"He was good and kept his distance."
"He was excellent, on the same wavelength."
"His confidence in us grew."
"She was very considerate, a good adviser."

'There are always adverse comments; these too are listened to very carefully. Notably this year, they seriously concerned only the problems arising from observation in large groupings. Others, a small minority, referred to what seems a long day with few of the usual school breaks or opportunity to change into less formal clothes.'

A LEADERSHIP COURSE FOR CCF CADETS

In 1981 D.J. Whittaker of the Combined Cadet Force at Haberdasher Aske's School in Hertfordshire produced a tutor's manual based upon the one I wrote originally for the Industrial Society in 1969. The introduction stated:

'Its aims are to teach the cadets about the nature of leadership and how it affects them particularly the responsibility it puts on them.

'The subject is set in a wide context and the ideas can be applied to industrial as well as military use, or indeed to a team game situation.

'The course starts by an analysis of leadership and develops towards the concept of Action-Centred Leadership. In this they are taught what leaders should do in particular situations. This idea sets the tone for the course, which should be participatory. Although some of the ideas will have to be given in the form of lecturettes, this must not dominate. The value of the course is to convince them of the ideas through discussions and practical exercises, and to make them think about leadership problems.

'There is a detailed discussion on application of certain key functions of leadership. This is followed by sessions on leadership styles, decision sharing, job satisfaction, responsibility, and skills of persuasion.

'Many of the ideas are obvious, but often need to be said. It is hoped that a person will become a more effective leader if he thinks about them. The tutor must set an example by his actions throughout the course.

'I should like to thank H.M.S. *Royal Arthur* and the Industrial Society for the information and ideas I obtained from them. These ideas, coupled with my own experience, form the basis of this course.'

In this context it is worth recording that the Officers Training Wing of the Royal Marines in 1979 presented a two-day leadership training programme at Pangbourne College and Elizabeth College, Guernsey. According to Colonel Commandant 'the programme was extremely well received and return visits have been requested. The viability of this programme and its usefulness have, I feel, been proved. Such a programme is an extremely effective way of putting over a leadership message. Genuine enthusiasm is generated for the subject being taught and for the Royal Marines.' He proposed that the programme should be continued for three schools a year—all that the Officer Training Wing could realistically undertake.

As an extension of its leadership development work with head teachers, the Industrial Society has begun to run ACL courses for pupils. Cheltenham, Oundle, Gordonstoun and the Cathedral School, Wells, were among the first to do so in 1985, followed by seven other schools in the next academic year.

Leeds Girls' High School introduced a packaged form of the Action-Centred Leadership course for the lower sixth pupils in 1987, changing certain exercises and substituting school-based ones. 'We had reservations about it at first, thinking that pupils still at school didn't have enough experience to gain much from it. I am delighted to say that we were quite wrong,' wrote Mrs. E.M. Higgins, organizer of the Industry Liaison Course at the school. 'What we are particularly pleased about is that it is helping them to look at their responsibilities and their life in the sixth form in a much more mature way.'

LEADERSHIP TRAINING IN THE SCOUTS AND GUIDES

The first leadership course I designed and led was actually for Scout patrol leaders. It took place in 1955. Like many things it seems to have happened by chance. Bernard Gadney, who had captained the English rugby football team in a famous victory over the All Blacks (the last before 1984), had founded a boys' school in Yorkshire of which he was the headmaster. We became friends and Bernard asked me if I would like to earn some money in the university vacation by doing some teaching there. Bernard was a keen scouter and I was recruited as a temporary assistant scoutmaster. The leadership course for patrol leaders was based upon rudimentary functional lines (it was long before I had come upon the three circles). It included a bridge-building exercise over the river that danced over rocks through a wooded valley in the grounds. The day culminated, I recall, with a night exercise in which —dressed in my Arab Legion clothes and armed with a starter pistol —I played the part of an intruder while the patrol leaders and their patrols observed and reported on my activities. After it was all over, the scouts drank gallons of hot cocoa into the early hours of the morning and exchanged boasts. Baden-Powell would have approved!

The present Chief Scout, Major-General Michael Walsh, served on the staff at Sandhurst when functional leadership training was being developed. In the Scout Association the leadership training syllabus for both the scout leaders (adults) and patrol leaders is based upon the three circles model and the functions of leadership approach. Although I have had no direct involvement in that story

— it was all taken from my books — I have been much impressed by what I have seen of scout leader training in Surrey, my home county, where I have now been made a member of the Surrey Scout Association's Council.

My links with the Guides have been even more tenuous. In 1968 I ran a leadership seminar at the large Guinness Park Royal Brewery in London. The chief statistician there was also the doyenne of trainers in the Girl Guide movement, and she invited me to speak to the national conference of the 'trainers of trainers'. Much later, in the 1980s, I ran some sessions for the West Surrey Guide leaders conference. There is no doubt in my mind that the Scouts and Guides movement do already make a very considerable contribution to developing tomorrow's good leaders — and leaders for good.

LEADERS OF TOMORROW

Adults are only too partial to the sorry task of warning youth that some day they will view most of the things that now inspire their hearts and minds as mere illusions. But those who have a deeper experience of life take another tone. They exhort youth to try to preserve throughout their lives the ideas that inspire them. In youthful idealism man perceives the truth. In youthful idealism he possesses riches that should not be bartered for anything on earth.

Albert Schweitzer

KEYPOINTS

- You learn a lot at school about leadership by observing the teachers at work and experiencing at first hand the effects of their good — or not-so-good — leadership.
- A good school will create a variety of opportunities for students to lead groups or teams, some with supervision (and feedback) from a staff member and some without.
- The ethos of the school, as established or maintained by the head teacher, should reflect a high value placed upon good leadership and leadership for good.
- Leadership training courses or conferences — using the outdoors — can play a valuable part within an overall strategy for developing the transferable personal skills of school children.
- The involvement of managers and their equivalents from the world of work, together with work experience, gives a wider significance to the principles and practice of leadership.
- The auxiliary contribution of such organizations as the Scouts and Guides is especially significant in the field of developing leadership and teamwork.

> *Some of the best moments in life are not when you have achieved something but when the thought first comes to you to have a go.*
>
> *Lord Hunt*

8 Case Study: The Prefect System Goes Comprehensive

The price of greatness is responsibility.

Winston Churchill

Getting the Structure Right — the eighth principle of developing effective leadership — applies to schools. In this context it means ensuring that there are real opportunities for pupils to exercise leadership in the school structure. The prefect system is the traditional method of providing those opportunities.

The prefect system, however, is not an infallible method of developing leadership. A public school housemaster wrote to me some thought-provoking words on the subject:

> 'May I suggest if you write any more books or articles on management that you devote some attention to the opportunities for management training in schools?
>
> 'I make this suggestion because, however effective the introduction of new attitudes and techniques in industry may be, schools are still generally operating on the basis of outworn attitudes. This is to be seen in the prefect system which used, perhaps rightly, to be regarded as a good preparation for management. What has happened is that, whereas business and industry have developed in a new direction, schools have, generally speaking, stayed put. Not so long ago schools and industry shared common assumptions, but they no longer do so. There are various reasons for this, e.g. public schools attract a fair number of people who do not like the changes that are taking place in society and they reinforce the conservatism of outlook especially of the more prestigious schools. But whatever the reasons

schools are not responding to the "winds of change" and I don't think they will until someone who speaks with a note of authority encourages them to.

'One of the problems is that for guidance in matters of schoolboy/girl authority patterns even comprehensive schools look albeit unconsciously at what goes on in boarding schools and this usually means public schools. I have set up an exchange scheme between boys in the House and a comprehensive school... The prefect system in the comprehensive school is impressively authoritarian and seems to reflect none of the attitudes underlying practice in modern industry: this in the industrial heart of England of all places!

'All this might not matter very much because when boys and girls go into industry they will be taught how management is done. But it would surely be better if the experience of authority and of management in schools was a genuine preparation for conditions in the adult world. It used to be so and I see no reason why schools should not base their authority structure on the same kinds of assumptions as the rest of society — as used to be the case. It is surely wasteful if, as at present, children have to unlearn what they have learned at school to enable them to adjust to what is practised in industry. At the moment, schools, especially the public schools, are encouraging fake expectations.'

In an attempt to swing away from he called the traditional 'authority structure' some schools have experimented with the elective approach. Richard Boult of the Industrial Society makes this comment upon it:

'An interesting development was that some schools who see themselves as progressive were inviting the pupils to elect their prefects. However, they then discovered that the prefects saw their role almost exclusively in terms of representing the views of pupils to the Head rather than representing the Head or taking part in the executive management of the school. They were in fact acting as shop stewards not as managers.'

Leaders can be appointed, elected or emergent. As I have pointed out elsewhere, there are important differences between these kinds of leaders. If leaders are elected they tend to feel responsible — if they are not actually accountable — to those who elected them. If tasks or responsibilities are given to groups the leader is usually appointed. He or she is accountable to the authority who appoints. Whether elected or appointed or both, a leader should be the sort of person who would emerge naturally.

A Norfolk head teacher, Michael Leigh, chose the development of the prefect system when I invited him to contribute to this book. He has now left Great Yarmouth High School to take up an appointment as County Coordinator of the Training and Vocational Education Initiative Extension (TVEI) in Norfolk, a potentially most interesting and exciting curriculum project.

'TVEI Extension, as you know, is intended to enhance and enrich the curriculum of 14 to 18 year olds in a manner which renders their education to be more relevant to their personal needs and those of society in the next decade,' writes Michael Leigh.

'It is not intended that this principle of relevance should be confined to technical education, although that will inevitably play a significant part in the initiative. We will clearly be interested in developing the personal qualities of our young people. As you will see from the notes which are attached, I am convinced that an element of leadership education would form an appropriate part of our scheme.'

THE PREFECT SYSTEM: A CASE STUDY

'In September 1981 Great Yarmouth Grammar School's 430 years of existence came to an end. Great Yarmouth High School came into being. As the forty-second and last Headmaster of the grammar School, and the first Headmaster of the new comprehensive school, I determined to carry some of the best features of the old school into the new.

'The grammar school had maintained a prefect system throughout the years. Until relatively recently this meant that a select group of upper sixth formers were appointed as prefects — about 20 to 30 in all. This 'hero' group was characterized by the following features:

1. It had a disciplinary function, keeping order at the beginning of assemblies, when teachers were late for

lessons, maintaining a watch on the school gates, and checking on individual pupil behaviour.

2. It could impose punishments, detentions and lines.
3. It was admired from a distance by younger pupils.
4. Its pastoral function was much less important than its disciplinary function.
5. Selection to the group depended upon factors such as academic ability, prowess in games, and general uprightness.
6. "Rough diamonds" and students with a chequered history in the school tended to be eliminated.
7. The function and authority of the prefects was invested in the system. Younger pupils did not question the system, although prefects always felt that they had less authority than their predecessors.

'Staff opinion was divided on the prefect system. A small group at one end of the spectrum, the Levellers, favoured the abolition of the prefect system altogether. At the other end of the spectrum, the elitists fought for the *"ancien régime"* — they wanted increased powers for more select groups.

'Between these two extremes were the social democrats. They considered that the traditional selection method was haphazard and was based on inadequately worked out criteria. Good potential leaders were overlooked if they had displayed too much spirited individualism. The nice, clever conformist who may have few effective qualities of leadership tended to be favoured. In any case, enquired the social democrats, how could you make judgements on leadership qualities without first having provided the student with the opportunity to exercise authority? Moreover, it was argued, if the object of the exercise is to *educate* young people in the exercise of responsibility, why should we deny the opportunity to some?

'Latterly therefore, it was decided to appoint *en masse* as prefects the entire upper sixth form of 60 students. The result was that some unexpected successes emerged. Inevitably, also, students were appointed who enjoyed the status without being willing to shoulder the responsibilities of prefects. Others wanted the status even less than the responsibilities, although surprisingly no one refused the title.

'As year succeeded to year, it became more and more clear that an increasing number of seventeen and eighteen year old students had become disenchanted with the exercise of authority over younger pupils. They felt that they had outgrown that sort of thing.

COMPREHENSIVE REORGANIZATION 1981

'A combination of several factors led many people to believe that the exercise of student leadership would not continue in the new school. A huge turnover in staff, and a dramatic increase in student numbers, brought an abrupt end to assumptions and traditions which had existed for years. The amalgamation of four schools and the arrival of large numbers of students who felt little loyalty or commitment to their new school brought into question the concept of corporate spirit which is the essential environment for a flourishing prefect system.

'It was the imminent departure of the sixth form to a Sixth Form College which was seen as being the final nail in the coffin of student leadership.

'Against this background, the decision was taken in 1981 to appoint fifth year students as prefects. Pupils were invited to apply by letter at the end of their fourth year stating why they wanted to be prefects. Each applicant was interviewed by a senior member of staff and form tutor. All members of staff were invited to comment on the suitability of each applicant. There were usually over 100 applicants (out of a total year group of 240). Usually 60 to 80 were appointed.

'Each year a small group of senior prefects were appointed – Head Boy, Head Girl, Deputy Head Boy, and Deputy Head Girl. A great deal of trouble was taken in choosing the right students for these posts. The retiring senior prefects were expected to display real leadership. They led and deployed their team of prefects; they represented the school on formal occasions; they were consulted and involved in matters of school policy. In the first year of comprehensive reorganization, no boy was willing to take on the task of Head Boy; in the second year we made a spectacular mistake in the appointment of Head Boy. Apart from that, the senior prefects responded magnificently. Some of them were quite outstanding.

'All prefects were expected to set a good example to the rest of the school both in appearance and in their personal behaviour. With one or two exceptions (who were demoted during the course of the year) all responded well to this minimum requirement in a surprising way. Additionally, prefects were appointed to junior forms, where they assisted form teachers. Some took on responsibilities in specific areas of the school, for instance in games, stage lighting, music, and community work.

* * *

'Perhaps all this seems to be unexceptional and conventional, and so it is. However, it was most interesting to observe the effects of changing school structures, changing age groups, changing social mores, and changing staff attitudes on the exercise of leadership by students in Great Yarmouth. Here are some of the consequences:

- Fifth year students proved to be as keen to take on the responsibilities of prefectship, as sixth formers had been reluctant. Many eighteen year olds felt that they had outgrown this brand of leadership, whereas many sixteen year olds had real appetite for such responsibility.
- A few fifth year prefects displayed qualities of maturity and leadership which were equal to those demonstrated by the finest upper-sixth formers.
- The majority of fifth formers felt more at home with the more mechanical aspects of responsibility. They were perhaps less confident in taking initiatives.
- Fifth year prefects felt more at home in a caring/protective role rather than in a disciplinary role. There were good reasons for this:
    a) The new prefects were closer in age to their charges.
    b) A higher proportion of their charges found it difficult to accept the authority of older pupils. Changing social attitudes, home backgrounds which were less authoritarian, and a situation where respect

had to be earned rather than assumed, all made the exercise of responsibility a more difficult task.

- Some prefects showed great courage in exercising leadership with difficult pupils.
- Some of the most impressive prefects were those who were not academically able, who had to fight against difficult home backgrounds, and who were themselves “rough diamonds”.
- Many prefects were being expected to shoulder responsibilities at the age of 15/16 in a way which would not be expected of them for several years to come.
- Some staff felt that too many prefects were being appointed and that too many were consequently “letting the side down”.

* * *

‘The exercise of leadership is never easy. Judgement has to be exercised, hard decisions have to be made, unpopularity has to be tolerated. The leader is often expected to work harder, to behave better, to run faster, to think more quickly, to feel less pain etc. than those who are led. It is not an easy task even when structures are clear cut, when authority is accepted as a matter of course, and where there are recognized lines of deference.

‘In the Armed Forces, great corporate businesses, the Police Force, the Civil Service, and probably in most public schools, the organizational structure, tradition and ethos all support the concept of hierarchy, authority and leadership.

‘In the contemporary comprehensive school this is often not the case. Here the concept of leadership is far more ambiguous. The pupil who is given responsibilities is not protected by tradition, by a cultivated mystique, by a deferential society, by a corpus of sanctions, by physical separation from his/her subordinates, or by an organization which underlines the leader’s authority.

‘In these circumstances, the leader must be far more flexible than might otherwise be the case. It may even be that the qualities required are akin to those required of the young lieutenant on patrol in the streets of Belfast. Sensitivity, resourcefulness, vigilance, restraint, persuasion, compassion, and the ability to think on one’s feet, are all necessary for survival.

* * *

'Recent research has indicated, not surprisingly perhaps, that employers look for two main attributes in potential recruits. Evidence of academic attainment in general education is their first priority; the second requirement is a range of personal qualities, including that of leadership.

'Is there not therefore a case for including an element of leadership education in the personal development programmes offered in British schools and colleges? Such an element should take account of the following issues:

- The need to interpret leadership in a broad way, to include leadership in the community. The principle of service would be an essential aspect of this interpretation.
- The possibility of cooperative ventures between institutions should be kept in mind.
- The opportunities offered in various types of residential experience are valuable.
- Records of achievement should take account of these qualities.
- Such organized activities as the Duke of Edinburgh Award Scheme all have much to offer.

'The encouragement of leadership qualities in pupils and students in our maintained schools and colleges is hugely important. Not only is it of personal significance to individual students, it is also vital if we are to remain a coherent and effective society.'

KEYPOINTS

- The principle of getting the structure right has several applications in schools. Creating real opportunities for people to lead and manage is one of them.
- The prefect system has often been rejected by staff and pupils alike because it has been seen as an apprenticeship for becoming a hierarchical boss. Properly interpreted, it can become an introduction to responsible leadership.
- No school should rely solely upon the prefect system for leadership opportunity. For those chosen to be prefects will more often than not be the boys and girls who are already on the way to becoming leaders.
- The method of asking for applications from those who would like to be prefects, and then appointing after consultation, has much to commend it.
- Prefects should receive some training in leadership, if they have not done so already, together with some guidance — not least from the hard-won experiences of last year's prefects. They should meet together regularly as a group to improve their contribution, having been briefed and consulted on matters of policy concerning the running of the school.
- New vistas are opening up for training in leadership and teamwork in schools.

> *You will have certain privileges; don't abuse them. You will have certain responsibilities; don't shirk them.... You must beware of over-officiousness towards those who are not your friends. A little authority is a dangerous thing. So walk warily at first.*
>
> *Ian Hay, 'The Lighter Side of School Life'.*

9 Case Study: Leadership Training for All Employees at Scott Ltd.

'We are going to win and the industrial West is going to lose: there is nothing much you can do about it, because the reasons for your failure are within yourselves.

'Your firms are built on the Taylor model; even worse, so are your heads. With your bosses doing the thinking while the workers wield the screwdrivers, you're convinced deep down that this is the right way to run a business.'

Konosuke Matsushita, Tokyo 1979

It is rare in the field of leadership training — as in any other — that there is a quantum leap forwards. Usually it seems breathtaking, simple and even obvious when it happens. The decision of Scott Ltd to give all their 800 or so employees at Northfleet the opportunity to attend an ACL course comes in that category. Why? Because hitherto we have always reserved leadership training for those who were occupying — or soon to occupy — leadership roles, which in industry are usually labelled 'management'. We have neglected the fact that everyone at work needs to be a leader in some way or other. Nor has the power of ACL as a vehicle for training team members and colleagues — not just leaders in formal roles — ever been properly utilized.

Philip Mansfield, the author of this case study, is the training manager at Northfleet. He used 'The Leadership Programme', a packaged form of ACL, as the basis for the 40 courses run at Northfleet in 1987. I will leave him to tell the story.

* * *

'Scott Limited, a company originally formed as Bowater-Scott in 1956 by a 50/50 partnership between Scott Paper Company of America and the Bowater Paper Corporation UK, is a paper company solely manufacturing toilet tissue paper and towelling products for both the domestic and industrial and medical markets. The company currently employs some 2,900 people, mainly at two manufacturing units at Northfleet in Kent and Barrow-in-Furness in Cumbria. Company turnover in 1986 was £211 million. Scott Paper Company became the sole owner in August 1986.

'As a company in about 1984 we began to feel the strong effects of competition from both new product ranges in this country and also from the European community. To combat this competitive challenge the company launched into a major capital investment programme during 1985, spending some £40 million installing new equipment and processes at both of the mills.

'It was quickly realized, however, that investment was only half the answer; our product cost to the customer was still too high. Negotiating crewing levels on the new equipment, developing a new charter agreement and introducing a redundancy programme: all these steps brought about a perceived adversarial management style within the Manufacturing Division.

'The Division soon decided this state of affairs was not going to bring the results we required and it was decided to look into ways to gain more commitment from all members of the workforce. With this in mind a meeting of the top 40 managers in the Division was held. As a result of it the Mill Managers then set about implementing new initiatives to bring about more involvement by the workforce. The Northfleet Mill management team decided to develop a "team" approach such as had been successfully operated in one department during the investment programme. To encompass the whole mill the management decided on the implementation of a four-point plan:

- Devise and communicate mill objectives.
- Develop a simplified "management by objectives" scheme that aligned the mill objectives to both departments and individuals.

- Introduce an incentive scheme based on a reduction in cost/case to the customer.
- Implement an Action-Centred Leadership programme that would include all those mill employees who wished to participate.

'The main thrust of the training department was the ACL programme. The training method used was an external package tailored, with consultant support, to meet our particular needs.

'The consultant trainer carried out the initial five two-day courses which began in April 1986, and during that time trained an internal trainer. This was done to develop "home ownership" as soon as possible. The first three courses covered the top 39 managers in the mill and to date 40 courses have been run. So far 556 mill personnel have attended out of a total of 893. Of that number, some 327 have been tradesmen and machine operators.

'Emphasis has been put on consistency of programme. All participants, whether management or workforce, have had exactly the same experience and all have received similar workbooks and handouts.

'Like all ACL courses, ours was designed to be as participative as possible. Discussions take place at each session, in both plenary and small groups, and two tasks are performed — one task is theoretical in nature and the other practical. The course concludes with a buffet and drinks session where senior managers join the group to answer any questions or queries and generally discuss the ACL concept.

'Difficulties in introducing the training were primarily logistical ones: deciding on the most convenient two days in the week that were compatible with the various shift patterns used in the mill was one principal problem. Other difficulties were making sure there was a cross section of participants from all areas of the mill. That was overcome to some extent by an allocation system, but now we are nearing the end of the programme that system is becoming more difficult to apply.

'Obviously, it was important in order to maintain impact to get everyone through the programme as quickly as possible. This has not being easy owing to the numbers involved. Already additional ways of involving people and further training are taking place to improve communication and technical skills across the mill as a follow-up to the course.

'After some initial discussion, 70 per cent of the trade unions representatives have attended courses and provided support to the programme.

'With developments of this nature it is difficult to provide tangible and quantifiable benefits, or to assign to the ACL training programme the true proportion of the performance benefits that are being perceived, not just by participants within the mill but also infrequent visitors. Some of these benefits:

- Employee involvement has resulted in substantial saving, nearly half a million pounds in one instance.
- Improved mill performance figures.
- Noticeable improvement in morale.
- All employees are far more aware of costs of down-time, waste, etc. and prepared to provide ideas on how to improve in these areas.
- Better liaison between departments and disciplines.
- Employees thinking more about the mill, the company and the papermaking process.

'We believe that what we are doing at Northfleet is exceptionally effective because we are developing people at all levels within the mill and providing them with more opportunity to be responsible for their own actions. This, we feel, must improve the quality of their working life and develop pride in their achievements.

'The company now views its people as its most important asset and values them as such. The Northfleet Mill is in the forefront of a company change of culture, moving from a controlled workforce to a committed workforce. Our ACL training has preceded a now bigger management development programme that has started to be implemented throughout the whole company. All the training that has been done and which is continuing, as it spreads across the company, will greatly support this new philosophy of management.

'We do not claim a 100 per cent success rate in this training. Both management and workforce, in some cases, find the required attitude change difficult. But we do claim a major cultural change in the mill towards a far more positive environment, where things happen with much more commitment.'

* * *

EVALUATION

The following comments come from tape-recorded interviews with course participants:

'I feel that the operators now feel more open, that they can talk to the staff and managers. Communication between departments is also much better.'

'Yes, I feel now that the operators feel a lot more involved, they know what's going on in the company more — the financial side and also they know what's happening outside a lot more. Marketing come down and they inform us what their plans are, what's taking place out in the market and what they're going to be looking for in the future, which makes the operators feel much more involved.'

'Now that the operators have been on the Action-Centred Leadership courses they feel that they are pushing up and they want even more involvement. They want their suggestions looked at; they want outsiders to come and listen to what they've got to say. I feel that it's now got to work down a bit from the management.'

'Everyone is being involved now. They're being informed within the department and everyone is beginning to work together.'

'We did go through a stage where we'd say "that's my job and I do it—it doesn't matter about anybody else!", but it's all altering now and people are getting involved.'

'You're getting everybody beginning to work together and therefore you pull together; you're not pulling against one another any more. You all see you're going the same way and you're heading for the same goal, whereas before you'd have some pulling that way and some pulling the other way. At least now we can see a goal, which in my eyes is a secure future and a secure job.'

'With these courses we've been having, these ACL programmes, and liaison meetings with our heads of department, hopefully we're beginning to work as a team or group rather than individuals who moan amongst themselves and don't really get the problem sorted out. As a group, we can all work together and make it better.'

'This Action-Centred Leadership course has been very good as far as I'm concerned and I think that quite the majority of the people that have been on the course have enjoyed it and have learned something from it. But I do rather think that the middle management, as far as I'm concerned, are not showing as much interest as they should be.'

'I think it is a step in the right direction to involve everybody, I'm only sorry we never had a course, or we never had the same feeling 20 years ago when I first came down here. I think things would be a bit different if we'd had that sort of thing 20 years ago, more involvement of workers, because I think you've lost a lot of talent, you've lost over it.'

'I think the firm will benefit from it and if the firm benefits from it surely to goodness everybody else is going to benefit from it. I can't see anything but good coming out of it if everybody pulls their weight and I literally mean everybody. You only get out what you put in.'

'Well, if we talk, everybody's got to talk, and get ideas and perhaps 99 per cent of the ideas are not viable, but surely there must be a few ideas that could come out of the shop floor or anywhere to be some good to the firm. You know from talking to your wife what they expect in the supermarket and that's how the goods should be put in there — we learn from them. We've got to consider the customer, the customer being ourselves — we are the general public and we should know what we expect to find in the supermarket and we should see that our goods get to the supermarkets in the condition that we expect to receive them.'

'Well, the benefits are that lots of people who maybe were frightened to say certain things are now voicing their opinions because they feel they are being heard and acted on.'

'If you want something specific, I can remember where we were taking ten minutes to load the reels onto the Perini, but through talking to everybody on the floor we managed to get a system in which now we use two hoists and the time has been cut down to four maybe five minutes and that's probably saved us half a million pounds over the system that was going to be introduced.'

'Yes, we have now liaison groups once every five weeks and people are working better as teams. We're getting to know each other — our strengths and our weaknesses — and people who are natural leaders. People are helping each other.'

'Well, on a personal level, I think you're getting the satisfaction of feeling more involved, rather than just coming into work to earn money. The company's getting ideas from people who are working the machines day in and day out and their knowledge, I think, has sometimes not been used as much as it can be. With regard to the customer, we are understanding more what the customer wants and we're looking for the faults and trying to rectify them before they get too bad.'

'I think we're getting more out because you feel you're being listened to now and I don't think that happened so much as it should have done in the past, so I think we can be stretched more. There is no God-given right of managers to have all the good ideas and it's nice to feel that an idea that you've brought forward has been used successfully.'

'Well, I personally feel more secure now. I know exactly what is going on. If I want to know what is being spent in the company or if new improvements are going to be made, I can go straight to the top man and he can tell me exactly what is happening. There is nobody I can't approach now in the company and ask for advice or opinions or anything else that I need to know.'

'I think the company will benefit from the point of view that more paper will be made, and the customer obviously will benefit. I think the quality is obviously going to be better. There is more thought being put into every action that is being taken and I think there are therefore big benefits for both the customer and ourselves.'

'Yes, what especially impressed us was a whole day out with the sales rep., going round, seeing the hard job he has to do, which surprised us. We usually see them (the product) going through the wall to the warehouse and that is it. Now we go beyond to the actual person buying the product. Seeing his hardships as well as ours has taught us that it isn't just making it, it's selling it that counts.'

'I just hope that we move on the way we've started, because it's obviously the way to go.'

THE MORAL OF THE STORY

There is an English proverb that says, 'There are no bad students, only bad teachers.' I believe it also applies to a company. There are no bad employees, only bad managers.

T.S. Lin
Chairman of Taiwan's Tatung Co. (1982).

KEYPOINTS

- Investing large sums of money in new machinery without investing in people is short sighted. It is people that run the machines and produce the goods.
- Everybody at work is a leader — or should be. We all have to lead ourselves: to develop a sense of purpose and to set high standards of craftsmanship and quality.
- Teamwork is essential in industry and commerce. Most people want to feel part of a team, contributing to a worthwhile common task.
- Leadership training for all employees is a unique recognition of each person's value as a contributor to the common enterprise.
- There are few better methods for identifying the problem areas in downwards, upwards and lateral communications within the organization.
- Leadership training at every level both helps to change organizational culture — so that all value highly the quality of the product and the all-important task of creating a satisfied customer — and is helped by it. 'The bird carries the wings, but the wings carry the bird.'

A business is the reflection of the people within it.

Roger Falk

10 Hidden Depths That Make A Good Leader

It is always the secure who are humble.

G.K. Chesterton

This chapter appeared as an article written in *The Sunday Times*, 18 May 1986.

The reason for including it here is that it reflects my growing interest in leadership development at the strategic level — and indeed at the grand strategic level. It was an attempt on my part to create a climate in which chief executives and senior directors would be more willing to participate in leadership seminars.

* * *

The former Labour prime minister, James Callaghan, had an admission to make during a recent lecture he gave. 'I've never felt required to make a systematic study of the art of political leadership — although, to be perfectly open, I might have been a much better leader if I had done so,' he said.

'When I was invited to speak on leadership,' he added, 'I read my first and only book on the subject.'

That a former prime minister should be willing to admit that he might have been a better leader if he had thought more and read more about leadership is very interesting. How many chief executives in industry, commerce and the public services would be willing to admit as much, if only to themselves? The barriers preventing their doing so are formidable.

The very fact that a person has become a chief executive may be taken as sufficient evidence that he is already a leader. Yet the occupation of a leadership role does not necessarily mean that the holder is a perfect leader and could not improve his or her performance.

What then is leadership? The qualities spring from the nature of leadership as contrasted with management.

Leadership starts at the top but it should not end there. The age of the autocratic boss, the one-man show, is over. There are too many leadership functions required to achieve the task, to build the team and develop each individual, for any single person to provide them all. Well-run companies today are guided by a team of leaders. This team itself needs a leader; that is the core responsibility of the chief executive.

But this leadership role should not be seen only by senior managers. Everyone in an organization needs to feel part of the team, contributing a talent. In order to do so, each team member needs to know the common purpose.

A chief executive must therefore be a communicator who is able to give all concerned an acceptable vision of what is to be done and why.

Communication means dialogue, and that implies listening as well as speaking clearly. A listening leadership is essential because each person in a business has at least one good idea on how to achieve the task better.

The British can be highly inventive and creative, but vast resources of intelligence, energy and experience are wasted because of poor leadership.

To get the best out of the British people requires more than management. Leadership is about inspiration; it makes us work harder and longer to achieve results which once seemed impossible. Leaders can provide this through their enthusiasm and through example.

Leadership is not always done from the front, nor is it always highly visible. But leadership without example in some shape or form is always defective.

One of our great misfortunes is that we imported from the United States several decades ago a number of misleading assumptions which the Americans are now busy discarding. The message then was that there existed a body of transferable knowledge, a so-called management science, that enabled anyone to run anything.

Chief executives infected by this idea tend to sit in their offices doing something they call managing, which is often little more than financial management and general administration. They cease to be visible at all. One British managing director expressed surprise to the chairman of Toyota at the amount of time he spent out of his office. 'Surely you should be spending more time at your desk managing the business,' he said. The chairman replied simply: 'But we do not make cars in my office.'

Being an effective chief executive today therefore requires leadership. The job description is to do with three overlapping responsibilities: to achieve the common task, to build teamwork and to inspire and develop individuals.

These central activities call for a pattern of intellectual abilities, practical experience and personal or social skills. Character matters far more than the management theorists ever imagined: inner strength and integrity, toughness combined with fairness, and a humanity expressed in warmth and humour.

How are these abilities and qualities developed? By experience? Yes, but experience without reference to principles is barren.

People find that it takes a long time to learn leadership by experience alone and the cost is often high. Young people in particular need leadership training. Providing it is done in the right way and at the right time, it reduces the time taken to learn by experience.

At the more senior level there is a need for opportunities to discuss the themes of leadership, communication and decision-making. In such forums chief executives should be able to take stock of their own practice of leadership.

Once again it is a case of leading by example.

11 Preparing for Strategic Leadership

It is better to begin in the evening than not at all.

English proverb

Traditionally leadership training has been confined to the ranks of junior and junior-middle levels of management or its equivalent, or those who aspire to those levels. (I am including supervisors in those levels.) The idea that those in the senior level of management might need some specific training or preparation for that role is relatively novel.

One reason for the neglect of training at or just below the most senior level in organizations could be the belief that leadership is no longer relevant at this level: what matters is money, money and money. The chief executive's role is seen more as financier than leader, making acquisitions or defending against unwelcome bidders, more at home in the merchant bank than on the shopfloor of his company.

It all depends on one's self-perception. A growing number of chairmen, managing directors and chief executives *do* see themselves in the strategic leadership role. But, as I said in the last chapter, they assume — or it is assumed — that they are leaders because they have got the job. To participate in a leadership programme would be tantamount to admitting that this was not necessarily the case.

Sometimes one only has to state assumptions clearly for their absurdity to be evident. Therefore I do not propose to argue the case. There is sufficient evidence in military and business history to show that success in leadership at the tactical and operational levels is no guarantee that one will be successful as a strategic leader. Alas, there is also plenty of evidence that it is possible to rise to the top of organizations or nations by means other than the demonstration of one's superiority as a leader.

DEVELOPING OUR DIRECTORS

Britain's top directors have learnt their management skills by relatively accidental, informal and badly organized processes of development on the job. This is the finding of a new Manpower Services Commission study called *Developing Directors – The Learning Processes (1987).*

This report is based on interviews with 144 directors in 41 manufacturing and commercial organizations. It says there are still organizations of significant size that make little or no attempt to plan the development of the people who will eventually take the most important decisions.

It also found that formal schemes of management development have been less successful than organizations believe and very few directors have had management training experience of four weeks or more.

The study also found that effective management development would occur more frequently if based on normal managerial work and at least some directors already in posts are prepared to consider and act on their own development needs.

The report says neither 'accidental' nor planned management development gives the whole solution. It recommends a new process of development — 'integrated managerial' or 'opportunistic' — by which managerial activities are used in an organized way to develop managers. This would take advantage of the normal managerial processes, but plan their use rather than simply allowing it to happen.

SOME EXPERIMENTS

Two five-day courses for senior managers have been introduced in recent years, one by Templeton College (the Oxford Centre for Management Studies) entitled 'Strategic Leadership' and the other by the British Institute of Management. Both have the merit of engaging well-known leaders from business to speak to the students. At this level, learning from the experience of chief executives, and hearing their thoughts on leadership and management, is an important ingredient in any course.

One weakness of both programmes, in my opinion, has been on the theoretical side. But that is obviously a matter for debate, and I do not wish to pursue it here. The main point is that a five-day course effectively rules out those who are already chief executives. Instead of being programmes designed for the top person, or those soon to be in the top job, these business school-type courses tend to attract senior managers, more at the operational than the strategic level.

There are, of course, other programmes for senior managers which do not have 'leadership' in their title. At one end of the spectrum, for example, the Institute of Directors organizes short courses (1-3 days) for directors; at the other end, again as an example, the Civil Service has introduced a mandatory long residential course in two parts for all those who are about to be appointed into the higher administrative grades. Business schools also have their offerings. America is ahead in this field; perhaps American senior managers are more orientated towards management education in general than their European counterparts. The American Management Association, for instance, has run courses for business presidents and vice-presidents for a number of years.

In 1986 two chief executives wrote to me for information about leadership seminars for them. Conscious of the total lack of provision in this area—the core of their role—I tried without success to persuade British institutions, such as the Manpower Services Commission and the National Economic Development Organization, to take up the challenge. For various reasons all declined. Therefore in 1986 I decided to go it alone and lay on such a course myself. (I learnt subsequently that 'course' was the wrong word to use. Like 'training' it smacked of too low a level. 'Seminar' or 'conference', I was told, are words — like 'development' — which are more acceptable to senior people.)

The course was entitled 'Leadership for Chief Executives' and it took place at Nuneham Park near Oxford. The brochure defined the aim as follows:

> 'The course is for chief executives, especially those within two years of appointment. Those shortly to become chief executives are also eligible for it.

> 'The aim of the course is to provide course members with the opportunity to study the nature and practice of good leadership in order to become more effective in their roles as chief executives.
>
> 'The seminar is designed for a small number of individuals drawn primarily from industry and commerce. It will be highly participative.'

The course lasted for a day and a quarter. (Earlier that year I had tried to mount a two-and-a-half days programme for chief executives without success.) The participants arrived in time for introductions over dinner, followed by a session working in pairs and in plenary on the question 'What is the role of a chief executive?' During the following day we explored the chief executive's major areas of leadership responsibility, such as strategic thinking and corporate planning, communication in large organizations, encouraging innovation and enterprise, the ten steps of leadership development (as in Part One), and effective time management.

The course was marketed by sending a letter and the brochure to the chairman or managing director of the top 600 companies in *The Times* list. About 200 companies replied. Of those who expressed interest the relatively short notice (about four months) ruled out some who were evidently keen to come. Some applicants fell more into the category of senior managers and so I had to decline to accept them. Ten chief executives signed up for the course, although in the end two dropped out at the last moment due to business pressures. Those who came were in charge of major industrial and commercial enterprises.

Beyond the letters I received after the course I have no means of evaluating this programme beyond my own judgement. One must be sceptical about what any seminar lasting little more than a day can achieve in terms of changing attitudes and imparting skills, but the participants clearly found it valuable to compare notes with their peers, with someone like myself acting more as a catalyst than as teacher or instructor.

SOME EXPERIMENTS

Behind the Nuneham Park course lay two pieces of action-research on my part. The first involved a study of the leadership of Bob Reid (now Sir Robert Reid), the chief executive of British Rail. He agreed to act as a guinea pig for the action-research project. I interviewed some 40 or 50 senior managers in British Rail and asked them — among other questions about leadership in British Rail — to identify Bob Reid's strengths and weaknesses as a leader. Then, as part of the leadership development programme — he was keen to lead by example — I gave him a profile of those perceived strengths and weaknesses. At the same time I conducted a similar exercise for the chairman and chief executive of a leading London merchant bank, Rupert Hambro of Hambro's Bank. In both cases I was also working on the strategic leadership development of the top management teams of directors. This happened by a combination of special sessions in the context of residential conferences and some meetings with individuals, ranging from single interviews to a series of three half-day tutorials.

The main conclusion I drew from the action-research exercise was that top leaders who know their own strengths and weaknesses as leaders are more likely to be effective than those who do not. The former, for example, are better at selecting people who bring complementary gifts or talents into the senior leadership team. The chances of significant personal change at that level are probably slight: it's more a question of making the best of what you are. Whether or not the 'best' in question matches up to the leadership requirements of the job will soon become evident to your colleagues and subordinates.

* * *

What was unique about the British Rail and Hambro's experiments was the initial focus upon the leadership of the chief executive. There are also some in-company programmes which set out to equip or train leaders at board level. Often they evolve from leadership training at junior and middle levels of responsibility. For example one of my main clients throughout the 1970s, Whitbreads, eventually invited their main board to participate in an ACL course: it sticks in my mind because one director was Field-Marshal Sir Richard Hull; he entered into the spirit of it and claimed to have learnt something from the day. Other companies, such as Bejams and Air Products, approached me to initiate their ACL programmes with a seminar or course for the board.

Such events, however, are more in the character of appreciations than courses as such. A more systematic approach is needed if an organization wishes to train its own directors and future chief executives in strategic leadership.

More recently I have organized and led a series of seminars on leadership — usually two and a half days in duration — for diocesan bishops of the Church of England and vice-chancellors of British universities. Elsewhere, in *The Becoming Church* (1976) I have described the 'staff college' course, lasting four weeks, that I developed for clergymen and ministers judged to be potential senior leaders in the Church of England and the Methodist Church while I was Director of Studies at St George's House in Windsor Castle. Some forty of these courses have now been held. About half of the members of the first course subsequently became bishops. During the 1980s I participated in a series of conferences on diocesan leadership, each attended by four or five diocesan bishops and their senior teams. About half of the dioceses of England and Wales have now participated.

ACADEMIC LEADERSHIP

The quality of academic leadership at every level, institution, faculty, department, is certain to be an issue of the greatest importance in the 1990s. It has already become so in the United States, but in Britain there has been a reluctance to emphasize leadership at the expense of collegiality. Yet the two are not necessarily in conflict. It is probably only by imaginative leadership that British higher education can maintain its independence. Vice-chancellors and directors may be the peak of the pyramid, but issues of leadership cannot be confined to 'top management'; they apply throughout institutions. Maybe particular attention should be paid to the choice of pro-vice-chancellors, deputy directors, and the rest of the second tier of management. Such appointments rarely generate the same excitement as those of vice-chancellors or directors. Yet the day-to-day management of institutions is in their hands, and they are people from among whom the top leaders of the 1990s will be chosen.

The Times Higher Education Supplement, 14.6.85

The first seminar on leadership for university vice-chancellors at Farnham Castle in 1985 followed that model, with teams from five universities participating. The second and third programmes in the series, which I also led, were open to all universities. They attracted newly-appointed vice-chancellors and pro-vice-chancellors. But they can do no more than highlight the nature and good practice of leadership in the academic field. Can any organization do more?

In the 1980s the International Thomson Organisation certainly tried to do more. It initiated a bold new approach to developing strategic leaders. Having heard about it I interviewed Sir Gordon Brunton, the chief executive, and Don Rose, then the personnel manager responsible for the programme. Don Rose has subsequently written an account of the approach in *A Handbook of Management Development* (ed. A. Mumford, second edition, Gower 1986) which I reproduce in part here.

CASE STUDY: THE INTERNATIONAL THOMSON ORGANISATION

'The first step was to organize a management audit of the top 250 managers across the organization — now seen as a group resource. With a succession plan and a fresh appraisal form to give the meetings discipline, the chief executive of each division was asked to come to group headquarters for one day each year to discuss the quality of his people. The most urgent problem that emerged was the selection and preparation of the next generation of main board directors.

'A group of fifteen senior executives were chosen from the management audit: managers with careers of solid achievement who had shown the ability to think about their businesses. They were judged to have the most potential to take on the role of director of the main board where the emphasis would be on strategy.

'As tutor to the group the Thomson Organisation coaxed Professor Douglas Hague to the Oxford Centre for Management Studies and paid his salary there (his only other commitment was to run the annual Strategic Leadership Course).

'Three three-day seminars were organized each year. One distinctive element in that programme merits attention. The group was asked to evaluate the organization's long term plan—its strategy. When the group was ready Gordon Brunton, the chief executive, and the current board sat in the hot seat and the group interrogated them about the thinking in the plan and its proposals (no restful experience). Arising from this we agreed that there were three aspects of the plan that needed more study. They divided into smaller groups and through the summer of 1982 the people worked away at these three topics. Douglas worked with the groups, bringing in experts who were able to give further advice where needed.

'When they were ready, they made their presentations to the main board. A depth of thinking and investigation was applied to topics of particular interest to the organization:

- The possibility of expansion in the Pacific Basin.
- The development of the organization's customer base.
- The policy for divestment.

'Five of the group were appointed later to the main board. A similar programme for potential divisional board directors has been done at Henley Management College.'

Don Rose summed up the experiment in these words: 'For the Thomson Organisation, what has been described above has been an adventure; an adventure in management development that is exciting and which abolished the boundary between the business school classroom and business — in essence a management development programme tuned finely to the needs of individuals and the business they are to manage.'

* * *

The success of the first Thomson experiment owed much to Sir Gordon Brunton, an outstanding business leader who had learnt much about the art of leadership from his mentor, Roy Thomson. It is fitting therefore if I conclude this case study with some words he spoke to his group's personnel conference in 1982:

> 'It is very important that we distinguish between leadership and authority. The acceptance of leadership is almost certainly a voluntary act of those who are led to those who lead. The exercise of authority is outside the realm of persuasion and is concerned with the exercise of power. Leadership has authority and power but authority does not necessarily have leadership.

'Over many years now I have observed with enormous interest, in fact almost with a sense of fascination — and I have been privileged to do so — those who hold very high positions in government and the trade unions, in business and in industry, and very many of them, indeed I would say the majority, have very great authority but they are not leaders.

'Let me now come closer to home and talk about Thomson's. Leadership is the most vital ingredient for our future growth and our future development. We have deliberately chosen a strategy which is based upon leadership and on talent and the success of our policy and, indeed, the very policy itself, depends upon our ability to develop the various levels of leadership.

'In saying that I think we must recognize the difference between management and between leadership. Leadership is obviously concerned with management but there are managers who are not leaders. I think one of the important differences is that a manager, particularly a functional manager, is and will continue to be involved in a specific sector or in a particular discipline, but to the leader there are no boundaries; he cuts straight across them either by sector or by company.

'This company has grown and has prospered from an entrepreneurial tradition of leadership and of management. Hopefully, that will be as great an asset in the future as it has been in the past but that is by no means certain. It is to find the leaders and the entrepreneurs of the future that we have set up the Strategic Managers Course and if, out of those fifteen people who are the top future talent of the organization as we discern it today, we can find one or two or three who can become leaders and entrepreneurs in the terms that I have tried to describe, then I think that our strategy in the years ahead will be in safe hands. If we can't then what we must do is to settle and develop a different strategy because it is those leaders who will make what we are currently trying to do possible. In terms of strategy ten years is not a long period of time...'

* * *

SERVE TO LEAD

Last month I was asked to walk the job at a company manufacturing ball bearings in Peterlee in County Durham. During my visit I heard from the employees that when they were working overtime on a Sunday afternoon the managing director came in and swept up the canteen. He was still a very powerful managing director who knew what was to be done and what was wanted, but he showed that, like all of us, he was an ordinary person as well.

To act as a leader and to involve people in their work is a grand and fine thing to do. All of us can do it if only we would practise whenever we get the opportunity, whether inside industry or in the local community.

John Garnett.

KEYPOINTS

- Every organization should take thought about how it can best help to develop potential chief executives.
- The ability to lead should be an essential prerequisite for appointment to the top job in times of change and uncertainty.
- Strategic leadership calls for the capacity to think strategically about the present activities and future direction of the business. It calls for a rare combination of personal qualities of character and mind, together with a broad-based experience of the business in question.
- An organization shows that it really value strategic leadership by investing in in-company programmes or development activities tailor-made for individuals of high potential. It will harvest good leaders for the lean years that may lie ahead.
- No one course or method of leadership training for chief executives has proved itself: more experiments are needed.
- If political leaders subjected themselves to some form of leadership training in their own sphere they would be setting a good example to those in the nation they are exhorting to be better managers!

If the trumpet gives an uncertain sound, who shall prepare himself for the battle?

Epistle of Paul to the Corinthians

12 Case Study: Applying the Ten Principles in ICI

We must obey the greatest law of change. It is the most powerful law of nature.

Edmund Burke

In September 1981 Bill Stead and Edgar Vincent—the two senior managers responsible for group personnel in ICI — came to see me at the University of Surrey. They gave me some background about the plight of ICI—1980 had been a disastrous year in which profits fell by 48 per cent and the dividend was cut for the first time since formation in 1926 — and told me that the executive directors had decided that the first priority in personnel strategy should be the development of what they called manager-leaders. They wished me to act as outside consultant.

My previous contacts with ICI had been few and far between. In the 1970s I knew it from afar as a company that had spent hundreds of thousands of pounds on hiring behavioural scientists, mainly American and some most distinguished, such as Douglas McGregor. Some innovations, for example the work on job enrichment, had had a high profile. It had a reputation for sophistication in its various management systems and management development programmes. Through the agency of the Chemical and Allied Products Industrial Training Board in the 1970s I spent a few days at ICI's ammonia plant on Teesside as co-trainer on a course for supervisors. That was about the sum of my knowledge.

Edgar Vincent asked me if I could suggest other organizations that had used my ideas to grow leaders, except the Army which he and his colleague had already visited. I remember being stuck for an answer. There were of course many organizations — some 2000 of them in 1981 — who were sending managers and supervisors on ACL courses, or even putting the whole management through an ACL programme but that was not the question put to me. I could think of no organizations that were *growing* leaders in the ways I had been recommending. I suggested that ICI might like to be the first real guinea-pig, and the pair of them thought that would be an excellent idea. They also suggested that in exchange such a project should prove an extremely valuable opportunity within the context of my own research into leadership and leadership development.

After some further discussions with Edgar, now Group Personnel Manager, we agreed upon a plan to get the ball rolling. Instead of my writing a paper on strategy or the board issuing a set of edicts it was decided that a major conference would be convened at Warren House, ICI's conference centre, at which a cross-section of able top managers in ICI's nine divisions could meet and discuss the matter, hearing from various specialists like me in the course of three days. Then it would be left up to them to identify the right strategy for ICI, and for their own divisions within it, in order to achieve the first of ICI's key personnel policies — the development of management-leaders.

THE WARREN HOUSE CONFERENCE

The Warren House conference took place in January 1982, based upon a programme that Edgar and I had worked out together. As consultant I was present throughout. I also gave one talk about the functional approach to leadership, together with some reminders about the contribution of Maslow and Herzberg, and the importance of understanding the decision-making continuum. Apart from the personnel director and chairman of ICI, the other speakers were Peter Prior (chairman of Bulmers), David Gilbert-Smith (Leadership Trust), and Andrew Stewart (a psychologist and independent management consultant who spoke about methods of selecting or assessing leaders).

Since my initial meeting with Edgar and his colleague, ICI had appointed in November a new chairman from among its three deputy chairmen — not the one that had been mentioned to me as the most likely. Edgar evidently regarded his appointment as a considerable bonus to the enterprise of leadership development that we were engaged upon. I met John Harvey-Jones for the first time in the bar at Warren House that evening (27 January) and he spoke to the conference informally after supper.

The chairman began by saying that ICI was wrongly positioned in terms of where its hardware was, its types of products, and its overcapacity in some areas. Above all it was not well positioned in the real growth markets of the Far East and USA. This picture had implications for management style/leadership pattern. 'We have first class management,' he said, 'but it has become excessively bureaucratic and political. We've adopted a value system that is ponderous, negative, unanxious to share risk and not willing to give headroom.

'What's the pattern for the next ten years? Instability and change will characterize it. It will be a repositioning decade, with lots of new patterns and shifts of power. Growth, as we've known it, will be greatly reduced. No company can exist without growth, therefore we have to make it by pinching the markets of competitors, outdating his products and developing new ones,' John Harvey-Jones continued. He talked some more about how he saw the emergence of some giants in the chemicals industry in Europe, a pattern like the one in America. Technologically we were in for enormous change.

'What do we need to work in this environment?' he next asked. 'A new attitude to risk — we minimize risk, we don't maximize opportunities. But the biggest risk of all is to take no risk. We have to be flexible, because we won't read the future right. We need to have an ability to move fast, more market sensitivity, more openness and trust, greater tolerance of differences and more courage in dealings with others. Individuals have the answers, not ICI as a group.'

John Harvey-Jones then turned to his work plans after he became formally chairman in April. He would start at the top with the board. 'Let's meet in the middle. We haven't got time for a slow trickle-down.' 'Double-guessing would be cut out by having fewer people — the size of the board would be reduced for a start.' The discussion that followed was exceptionally frank on all sides. In response to one question the chairman pointed to 'the catalytic things we can do' to encourage entrepreneurial enterprise. 'The present ICI system will kill any business! The dynamic has been increasingly centralized. One of my jobs at every level has been to hold an umbrella over my chaps' heads. Senior management is about getting people to own the problem and to do something about it, not passing it up. Our system must be not to have a system.'

A sense of urgency coloured his closing remarks. It is a race against time — we are too late — the world is breaking up — bits to be grabbed now. His vision of an adaptable, open, flexible, fast-moving ICI — ready to move quickly in perceived thrusts or directions. 'We've got to grow this new ICI.' Asked about the attitude of his fellow directors he said that he couldn't order them. 'I have to lead the board to lead. They voted for me. There is no such thing as one leader. What matters most is a common sense of values. Leadership is about getting extraordinary performance out of ordinary people. In ICI we have got extraordinary people to begin with.'

In answer to another question John Harvey-Jones highlighted another strength. 'ICI exists through its ability to work informal systems. We have got the ability to work together informally. I'm keen on clarity of organizational responsibilities, but we've got to keep this informal ability to work together, because we'll never get the structure right. We start miles ahead of any other European chemical company; we have shown in the last two years that we can be unbelievably fast. We've got a lot going for us, such as a good technological basis. In other respects I could wish we were better placed. But we can knock the hell out of the opposition.'

Inspired by those words and determined to end the 'treacle', as they called it, which the ICI bureaucratic culture had created, the participants in the conference continued working all next day on their strategic action plans for liberating the leadership and enterprise within ICI.

LEADERSHIP TRAINING IN ICI

Among the recommendations each of the nine divisional teams resolved to introduce leadership training based upon the three circles approach — task, team and individual — which I had outlined. In keeping with the new emphasis on decentralization, it was left to the divisions to devise their own leadership training programmes, using me as a resource. My contribution varied accordingly. Looking through my diaries I see that I spoke to all the senior managers in one division; spent three days at Warren

House with all the finance directors and their teams; advised one division on its leadership course and did some on the spot 'training of the trainers' after the first one; did some counselling sessions with some divisional directors on an individual basis; advised four managers who had been asked to make recommendations on the key issue of leadership to the board of Organics Division; reviewed ICI's methods of selecting graduates; and carried out an evaluation survey of all the external leadership courses currently being used by ICI. But perhaps my most important contribution was to lead a one-day seminar each year for four years with Edgar Vincent for the nine divisional training managers responsible for the functional leadership courses in their various forms.

It is not within my compass here to say more about the radical changes that have taken place during the chairmanship of Sir John Harvey-Jones, which ended in 1987, especially as Sir John himself is writing a book on the subject. As I mentioned earlier, in 1984 ICI was the first British company to break the one billion pound profit barrier (the second, National Westminster Bank, has also made continual use of ACL since its introduction in 1969).

Of course the success of ICI in the period under review cannot be ascribed entirely to leadership, although I don't suppose that anyone would deny the importance of leadership as shown by Sir John Harvey-Jones and by many other ICI manager-leaders at every level in the divisions. As for leadership development, all that can be safely said is that it has proved to be not incompatible with business success.

> *Leadership is about getting extraordinary performance out of ordinary people.*
>
> *Sir John Harvey-Jones*

KEYPOINTS

- In 1981 the board of ICI accepted a key personnel strategy as part of its overall business strategy of repositioning and regenerating ICI. (The personnel director is one of the seven or eight directors on the main board.) That overall strategy has been successful: ICI is back among the world leaders in the chemical and pharmaceutical industries. 'Just as we need a business vision for the future we need a people vision too,' said Harvey-Jones in 1982 to the representatives of ICI's employees. Good selection procedure has ensured that ICI had a good supply of actual and potential manager-leaders.
- The main thrust of the new programmes in leadership training for managers and supervisors came within the nine divisions. All these programmes used the three circles model (p. 10) as the basis of their teaching about good leadership in management.
- Like all large companies ICI had faced the problem that divisions tended not to release people for career development purposes. However, it made substantial progress in that direction.
- The importance is stressed of managers knowing their people as individuals, dealing with them face-to-face and getting their support.
- A small 'research and advisory' team — the Group Personnel Manager and his divisional counterparts — guided the leadership training programme.
- Layers of hierarchy and scores of committees were scythed away in the division and at headquarters, where Harvey-Jones dispensed with two deputy chairmen and reduced the size of the main board. One divisional board was reduced from twenty directors to six. A rigorous policy of decentralizing decision-making authority and central services, such as purchasing and shipping, was followed.
- Much more emphasis was put on individuals using their own initiative and 'owning' their own self-development.

- In the 1970s ICI suffered from the problems of size. According to a senior ICI man 'It employed too many high paid people to check and cross-check other men's figures. It was an over-educated company. It had a technical bias, was not breeding people with entrepreneurial flair.' A new organizational climate has begun to emerge in which leadership can grow and flourish. The chairman's role was strengthened into that of chief executive (called 'principal executive officer' in ICI). As tenant of it, Sir John Harvey-Jones not only showed leadership by giving the company a sense of direction – 'I hope I am a leader but I'm not a one-man band' – but did all in his power to encourage it in others. He talked about it, placing it high in his list of values. He took part in training courses, and in one year met more than 8,000 ICI managers in group discussions.

> *How do you know you have won? When the energy is coming the other way and when your people are visibly growing individually and as a group.*
>
> *Sir John Harvey-Jones*

In Conclusion: The Way Ahead

The business of life is to go forwards.

Samuel Johnson

In PART ONE of this book I have presented the distilled experience of leadership development in the form of ten principles or steps. They are not in any order of importance: it is an *à la carte* menu, although I have argued that all the dishes should be eaten at some time or other. PART TWO contains the developments which have caught my attention, or in which I have been personally involved, in the field of leadership training. Like most adventurers I have felt the need to record the journeys I have been on, not least for the benefit of travellers that come after me.

Action-Centred Leadership, the standard course for managers and others which developed from the functional leadership course I evolved for Sandhurst officer cadets in the 1960s, is now international. The course has been successfully run in many countries of the world, mainly through the agency of the Industrial Society. Outdoor or adventure-based forms of the ACL course are now well-established in Australia and the United States. The three circles model has the merit of transcending cultural boundaries.

As I have stressed in this book, however, leadership development embraces more than training in the shape of courses, seminars or conferences. A growing number of organizations have now accepted this fact. There is a danger that they will wrap it all up in a new jargon, a mystique called management development. The development of managers can be totally systematized providing you hold a sufficiently impoverished concept of management. A higher concept of management, one which sees the role of leader as its core, takes you more into the realms of leadership development, the subject of this book. In that context system is only part of the solution: it takes leaders to beget leaders.

For no system as such can do more than contribute to the self-development or growth of natural leaders, men and women of sufficient stature to challenge systems, to transcend and transform the organizations that have in part shaped them. Management training done badly provides broiler-chickens, leaders without flavour. Leadership development by contrast should produce free-range birds or — to stretch the analogy — wild geese with vision, a sense of direction and the power of flight.

In PART TWO I have traced some developments of leadership training in the years before a young man or woman becomes employed, especially in the home and in the school. Home and school, youth organizations such as the Scouts and Guides, adventurous training and expeditions, church membership and youth clubs: all these have a contribution to make to the growth of leaders. Apart from the all-essential group experience — working as a team to complete tasks — these activities are opportunities for natural mentors — wise men and women who can help young people to identify and develop their gifts for leadership in the broadest sense. 'Confidence is a plant of slow growth,' says an English proverb.

As other chapters in PART TWO — concerning commanders in the Services, managers in industry and heads in schools — illustrate, the principles of leadership development have to be applied consciously and persistently. At least these principles have now been clearly identified, and they can be used for the purposes of analysis, diagnosis or organizational development.

A key challenge remains the development of leadership at — or just below — the strategic level. Most organizations need to develop leaders for the boardroom.

My other major concern is the training of trainers. The word amateur comes to mind when I contemplate it. Perhaps that is understandable if you remember that there has been virtually no money spent on leadership development, or provision for long courses for training the trainers — whereas many millions have been poured into management development (academic posts, research grants, management departments, colleges and business schools) over the last twenty or thirty years. Much of this money, especially in what purports to be research into management, appears to have been wasted.

Industry is the dominant institution of our times and management is part of its ideology. I know that the clock cannot be put back. But now that leadership is seen to be such an important part of management, especially on the edges of high achievement, the balance of investment between management and leadership (especially in the various fields of education) needs to be re-examined.

It seems only yesterday, but it was nearly forty years ago, since I gave my first talks on leadership as a boy as St Paul's School and then as a young officer cadet at Eaton Hall. Little did I realize then that leadership training and development would play such a large part in my life. This book now completes the trilogy of progress reports on the contribution that along with many others I have been fortunate and privileged to have made. More important, it points the way forwards for all who care about the growth of good leadership — and leadership for good — in our society.

There are times, I must admit, when I have wondered if any progress was being made. It has been actually reassuring to write this book and to see how much has been done. But the task that remains is still immense and the realities are that the resources devoted to leadership training will remain pitifully small. So much in this suffering world still demands a quality of leadership and teamwork that just is not there. Britain has a treasure in its unique tradition of leadership and leadership development which it is beginning to share with the rest of the world. We need such a market-place, where the world's ideas and experiences on how best to grow leaders can be exchanged and digested for the benefit of all.

Therefore there can be no resting. The story of education and training for leadership in a free and democratic society, a world that seeks to conquer the spectres of war, famine, disease, ignorance and want, is only just beginning.

> *There must be a beginning of any great matter, but the continuing unto the end until it be thoroughly finished yields the true glory.*
>
> *Sir Francis Drake*

Appendix A

(1) LEADERSHIP FUNCTIONS AT SANDHURST

• *Planning*	Seeking all available information. Defining group task, purpose or goal. Making a workable plan (in right decision-making framework).
• *Initiating*	Briefing group on the aims and the plan. Explaining why aim or plan is necessary. Allocating tasks to group members. Setting group standards.
• *Controlling*	Maintaining group standards. Influencing tempo. Ensuring all actions are taken towards objectives. Prodding group to action/decision.
• *Supporting*	Expressing acceptance of persons and their contribution. Encouraging group/individuals. Disciplining group/individuals. Creating team spirit. Reconciling disagreements or getting others to explore them.
• *Informing*	Clarifying task and plan. Giving new information to the group, i.e. keeping them 'in the picture'. Receiving information from group. Summarizing suggestions and ideas coherently.
• *Evaluating*	Checking feasibility of an idea. Testing the consequences of a proposed solution. Evaluating group performance. Helping the group to evaluate its own performance.

(2) FUNCTIONAL EFFECTIVENESS

DEFINING TASK	Correctly specifies what needs to be accomplished and breaks this task down into its discrete parts.
PLANNING	Formulates an effective method for achieving the task(s), i.e. organizes people, materials, time and resources in such a way that the objective(s) can be met.
BRIEFING	Allocates tasks and resources to subordinates in such a way that each person (a) knows what is expected of him and (b) understands the importance of his contribution.
CONTROLLING	Keeps things running to plan. Is sensitive to problems and delays and is quick to respond to them. Coordinates the work of the team.
EVALUATING	Makes accurate and insightful judgements about proposals, past performance and people.
MOTIVATING	Creates and maintains the team's commitment to, and interest in, the task.
ORGANIZING	Creates a structure and hierarchy appropriate to the task.
SETTING AN EXAMPLE	Exemplifies the values and behaviours he/she wishes to see in others.
SUPPORTING	Encourages group/individuals; builds and maintains good team spirit.

Appendix B

ORIGINS OF OUTDOOR LEADERSHIP TRAINING

The grandfather of all outdoor leadership courses was the 'No. 1 Leadership Development Training Centre' established by Sir Ronald Adam, the Adjutant-General, in 1943. (Its name was subsequently altered by Lord Rowallan, the first commanding officer, who established it in Scotland.)

In *Training for Leadership* (1968) I gave a short account and perhaps rather critical account of this innovative course. Lord Rowallan wrote to me after publication with some additional information. (See also Paul Harris, *Rowallan: The Autobiography of Lord Rowallan*, 1976 pp. 121-131.) He stressed the wider developmental aspect of the course — greater 'awareness' and the stimulus of interest and ideas as well as arousing latent initiative:

> 'I see you approve of our changes every ten days or so, to bring everybody into an entirely fresh environment. These changes were also used to separate 'the sheep from the goats'. The two men in each group who showed most leadership were removed from the common pool and distributed separately among the groups; and after the second move, those whose leadership was confirmed were put in a group of their own, partly to allow others to come to the top and partly to give them stronger competition. This segregation was repeated at each change and it was interesting that those who came to the top in the first two changes were generally those who were just good NCOs who stood still and were passed by others. It was also interesting that very often the unexpected suddenly blossomed and having reached the 'elect' they held their position...
>
> 'When I wrote you a day or two ago, I omitted my personal talks with individuals. At the beginning of the course I told them that we hoped to give them a taste of

many different dishes, but we did not want them to be tied down with discipline too strictly, but that there were certain standards which we should expect them to maintain....

'I interviewed as a routine matter every candidate, as we called them, at least twice during the course, giving them advice and encouragement. We kept things as informal as possible, pointing out that they had been chosen to come to us because they were responsible people. Our exercises in the hills gave the platoon commanders opportunities of chatting with the candidates and learning their approach to the course. Any criticism was given personally, and not in the presence of others. This personal relationship was invaluable in watching their development and progress.'

In the 1970s a company was established at Sandhurst for those who had just failed the Regular Commissions Board and named after Lord Rowallan. The candidates were given a twelve week intensive course, largely based upon the three circles and functional approach to leadership. The commanding officer of Rowallan company invited me to meet his staff soon after its inception. In later years the Rowallan Company has demonstrated amply that leaders can be developed. For example, one member of the company who had successfully passed into Sandhurst subsequently won the Sword of Honour.

As a personal postscript: one of the officers most involved in establishing 'No. 1 Leadership Development Training School' in Scotland in 1943 was General Sir Andrew Thorne, then the General Officer in command of Scotland. Rowallan, who had served in the Grenadier Guards during the First World War, named him as 'a great leader and one of the three great Battalion Commanders of the Grenadiers in 1918' (the others being Gort and Brook. Donald Lindsey has written a biography of him, entitled *Forgotten General: A Life of Andrew Thorne,* Michael Russell, 1987).

In 1970, while leading a conference on ACL at the Industrial Society's then headquarters in Bryanston Square, I noticed a spry septuagenarian listening intently. In the coffee break we met and I noticed the name 'General Sir Andrew Thorne' on his name label. When I asked him why he of all people should waste a morning coming to hear me, he replied with a smile, 'My grandson went through your leadership course at Sandhurst and was so enthusiastic about it that I decided to come and hear about it myself.'

Appendix C

TRANSFERABLE PERSONAL SKILLS

Some Definitions

A. *Leadership and Teamwork Abilities*

The ability to get things going — especially the ability to get people working well as a team towards a common goal.

Typical behaviours:

Sets direction and initiates action.

Plans and organizes.

Delegates responsibility.

Coordinates and controls.

Shows sensitivity to needs and feelings of individuals.

Motivates and encourages others.

Sets group standards.

Disciplines where necessary.

Seeks help and advice.

Plays positive role as team member.

B. *Decision-making Abilities*

The ability to think clearly in order to be able to solve problems and make decisions.

Typical behaviours:

Analyses problems.

Shows reasoning and logical thinking.

Is 'swift on the uptake'.

Thinks imaginatively and creatively.

Has a sense of reality.

Has 'helicopter' ability to stand back.

Demonstrates good judgement.

Has an inquiring mind.

Generates solutions.

Is decisive when required.

C. *Communication Abilities*

The ability to make points so that others understand them, and to comprehend the points that others make.

Typical behaviours:

Speaks audibly and clearly.

Uses simple and concise language.

Communicates on paper easily and well.

Listens to others with perception.

Reads with speed and comprehension.

Argues assertively but not aggressively.

Chairs a meeting well.

Ensures good group communications, upwards, downwards and sideways.

Shows awareness of non-verbal communication.

Gets others enthusiastic about his ideas.

D. *Self-Management Abilities*

The ability to manage your time effectively and to organize yourself well.

Typical behaviours:

A self-motivator — 'lights his own fire'.

Able to work on own initiative with little supervision.

Sets and achieves challenging goals.

Works to deadlines.

Makes good use of his/her own time.

E. *Personal Qualities*

The following qualities (in no order of merit) are mentioned as being of value by employers of graduates:

Strong but not dominating personality.

Personal impact, good appearance, poise.

Resilience, ability to work under pressure.

Flexibility and adaptability.

Energy and vigour.

Self-confidence or self-assurance.

Reliability, stability, calmness.

Breadth of interest.

Enthusiasm.

Integrity.

About the Author

Few individuals have had as much impact on leadership training as John Adair, author of *Training for Leadership* (1968). *Action-Centred Leadership* (1973) and *Effective Leadership* (1983). More than one million managers throughout the world have been through the Action-Centred Leadership (ACL) course that he pioneered.

John Adair is now internationally well-known as a writer, teacher and consultant. In 1978 he was appointed as the world's first Professor of Leadership Studies at the University of Surrey, where he is still a visiting professor.

This unique appointment followed John Adair's varied and colourful early career. After joining the Scots Guards he became the only national serviceman to serve in the Arab Legion, where he was adjutant of a Bedouin regiment. Before going to university he qualified as a deckhand and worked on an Icelandic trawler. He also worked as an orderly in a hospital operating theatre.

After Cambridge John Adair became Senior Lecturer in Military History and Adviser in Leadership Training at the Royal Military Academy, Sandhurst. Then, after two years as the first Director of Studies at St George's House in Windsor Castle, he became Associate Director of the Industrial Society.

The author holds the degrees of Master of Arts from Cambridge, Bachelor of Letters from Oxford, and Doctor of Philosophy from the University of London. He is also a Fellow of the Royal Historical Society.

John Adair is married with three children and lives in Guildford. He writes extensively on leadership and related subjects, as well as history. *Developing Leaders* is his twenty-first book.

Index